Sounds and Souls:
How music teachers change lives

Ruth Bonetti

Published by:
Words and Music
PO Box 422,
The Gap Qld. 4061 Australia
Phone (+61) 07 3300 2286
Mobile (+61) 0411 782 404
http://www.ruthbonetti.com

First edition, 2013
ISBN: 978-0-9578861-8-6

This book is copyright. Apart from any fair dealing for the purposes of private study, research, criticism or review as permitted under the Copyright Act, no part of this book may be reproduced by any process without the written permission of the publisher.

National Library of Australia
Cataloguing-in-Publication data:
Author: Bonetti, Ruth, author.
Title: Sounds and souls : how music teachers change lives / Ruth Bonetti ;
ISBN: 9780957886186 (paperback)
Subjects: Music teachers.
          Music coaching.
          Music--Study and teaching.
          Teacher effectiveness.
          influence (Literary, artistic, etc.)
Dewey Number: 780.7

Cover and internal design: Book Whispers www.bookwhispers.net
Printing: Lightning Source

Dedication

For two beacons who lit my voyage into music, teaching and indeed, life:
John Curro, for opportunities, vision and the challenge of 'Why not?'
David Shephard, who listened, encouraged, and whose sounds warmed my soul.

Acknowledgements

Just as a symphony performance blends intricate sounds and souls, to write this book was to weave a tapestry of experiences and people. We hear many voices other than mine, of colleagues who shared insights; they have been acknowledged where possible. Of students and their parents, many of whom remain friends long after lessons ceased.

The chapters about nurturing gifted students and handling criticism were first published in *Taking Centre Stage*, now out of print. There are strands of articles, blogs and eZines; some sections from earlier books bear repeating, like the perennial issue of rhythm, drawn in part from *Practice is a Dirty Word: How to clean up your act*.

Particular thanks for contributions and support are due to Dr Rita Crews, Cheryl Morrow and Julie Price. Also to Daniel Baxter, Tom Beek, James Cuddeford and Phil Davis. Thank you Debbie Terranova for reading the manuscript, Anne Hamilton for expert editing and Rochelle Manners for her expertise. To my health practitioner team who have helped me function through the years, especially naturopath Leanne Stockwell, and yoga teacher, Leanne Davis.

As ever, many thanks to my husband Antoni who has taught and played alongside me for many decades, and to my sons Paul-Antoni, Simeon and André. Sharing their lives and musical journeys has made me a more understanding, tolerant teacher.

Other books by Ruth Bonetti

Confident Music Performance: Fix the fear of facing an audience
ISBN: 978-0-9578861-6-2

Practice is a Dirty Word
ISBN: 978-0-9578861-5-5

Practice WAS a Dirty Word – Music Journal
ISBN: 978-0-9578861-2-4

Don't Freak Out – Speak Out
ISBN: 978-0-9578861-0-0

Enjoy Playing the Clarinet
ISBN: 978-0-19-322108-6

Enjoy Playing the Clarinet – Piano Accompaniments Book
ISBN 978-0-19-322109-3

Music Scales– Tips to make them happen
ISBN: 978-0-9578861-1-7

Speak Out – Don't Freak Out (eBook)
ISBN: 978-0-9578861-3-1

Clarinet Series 2 (AMEB Grades 1-4, Allans Publishing)

Contents

Acknowledgements	v
Preface	1
Introduction	3

TEACHER

Chapter 1	7
Teachers change lives	
Chapter 2	13
Qualifications and skills	
Chapter 3	16
School versus home studio	
Chapter 4	21
Running a Business	
Chapter 5	31
Teaching in schools and music shops	
Chapter 6	42
Stay Fresh with Stimulus	
Chapter 7	44
'Me Time'	

TEACHER—STUDENT

Chapter 8	58
First lesson, first impression	
Chapter 9	60
Choice of methodology and repertoire	
Chapter 10	63
Copyright and music in the public domain	

Chapter 11	66
What to cover in a lesson?	
Chapter 12:	69
Practice expectations	
Chapter 13	72
Tips for the time–poor	
Chapter 14	74
Motivate and Inspire Students	
Chapter 15	78
Understand Development Stages	
Chapter 16	84
Understand People to Motivate	
Chapter 17	89
Crowd Control for Group Teaching	
Chapter 18	91
Rhythm repairs	
Chapter 19	97
Note reading	
Chapter 20	101
Make technique palatable	
Chapter 21	104
Preparing students for examinations	
Chapter 22	107
Offer performance opportunities	
Chapter 23	112
Prime students to work with accompanists	
Chapter 24	116
Help for nervous students	
Chapter 25	119
Help Students to shine in performance	
Chapter 26	123
Help your students handle critiques and criticism	
Chapter 27	137
Retain Students	

Chapter 28   140
  When students resist change
Chapter 29   145
  Instrument issues
Chapter 30   150
  Communication and people skills
Chapter 31   153
  Sell the benefits of learning music
Chapter 32   158
  Special needs students
Chapter 33   165
  The gifted student

TEACHER – PARENT

Chapter 34   174
  Positive Parent Relations
Chapter 35   183
  Assert yourself with grace
Chapter 36   186
  Speak out with confidence in parent–teacher meetings
Chapter 37   189
  Your voice is your instrument–handle with care
CODA   192
Bibliography   195
Websites   198
Index   201

Preface

There is in souls a sympathy with sounds;
And as the mind is pitched the ear is pleased
With melting airs or martial, brisk, or grave:
Some chord in unison with what we hear
Is touched within us, and the heart replies.

William Cowper, *Winter Walk at Noon*

The following pages have evolved from my experiences of coaxing a range of sounds from a cross section of souls. Many tones have been pleasing; others close to agony. Decades ago I had to make an excuse to leave the studio, for my unborn baby expressed his personal opinion with some violent kicking. All students display individual qualities; some are more resistant to moulding than others.

At such times we can lose sight of the satisfactions of teaching. In our focus on rhythms and fingerings we can underestimate our words and actions, how the sounds we demonstrate impact on the souls whose lives cross ours. Our only clue might be when students are sad if we move state or country and write to us, hoping to visit. Twenty years later we should not be altogether surprised to discover they become professional musicians.

This resource in part traces my journeys across the years. Students have come and gone, some with heartwarming success and some with conspicuous lack of it. Yet whatever their progress, relationships were founded on empathy and sympathy. Even with the most frustrating students.

No two paths are the same, for teachers or for pupils. Thus, my experiences are not yours, but the anecdotes here may touch you with chords of 'Oh yes!' If so, there is worth in our shared knowledge. This personal voyage does not purport to weighty pedagogy. As I digested academic treatises to add ballast to my own ideas, I sensed there are needs beyond pedagogy. Those who steer an often reluctant crew through reefs of distractions need to stay afloat long enough to inspire and motivate students in order to retain them past shoals of over commitment. Teachers who work in relative isolation in home studios need to know they are not alone in their struggles against the tides. While there are aspects relevant to teachers in the classroom, a major focus is for studio instrumental teachers.

This book faces the realities teachers encounter. It seeks to stimulate and spark ideas: to empower and enliven the hurly burly times when we seem to give out more than we receive. To uplift with the knowledge that our teaching enhances and transforms lives. That the souls whose sounds we nurture are enriched by the music we share.

Introduction

We teach what we needed to learn.

Ruby would have been a challenge to any teacher. She had no natural rhythm at all. She could barely tell the difference between crotchets, quavers and semiquavers, but hoped a clomping foot tap would keep them on track. The foot slowed of course when passages looked almost black to her.

Aural perception? Intonation is a blur.

Harmonic understanding? Blank looks.

How would you meet this challenge? What would you do with Ruby? Pass her to another teacher? Suggest ballet? Casually mention to her parents they could save the cost of your tuition by enrolling her instead in a drama class?

Don't be so hasty. She may have hidden depths—or blocks. She is a slow developer.

I know. I was like Ruby.

My early piano lessons were from a governess who passed on her limited repertoire of *Fairy Bells*. If only subsequent teachers had taken me back to basics! Instead, when one pompous specimen heard a kookaburra outside, he sneered, 'Why, even the jackass laughs at you.'

From that point, my brain went into spasm when faced with a piano. The elderly Miss Quaver further alienated me with her wavery falsetto: 'D, dear, D. Where are my glasses? Oh yes, F dear.'

My struggles to coordinate two clefs and handfuls of notes going in different directions made me an unlikely contender for a future professional musician. The odds were slim, even before the first lesson.

I was reared in the Australian bush on hillbilly music. My first experience was with a jangly piano whose innards had been nibbled by mice. Its tone and tuning had been crippled by the searing heat and dust of the far west. Any concept of intonation was flummoxed for years later. My sister lowered my self-esteem by playing my pieces twice as loud and twice as fast. I found a way to fix that.

My life was changed by an Australian Broadcasting Corporation radio schools programme. The wind instruments came on in turn: 'This is the flute.' Tweet. *Nah.* The oboe: hmm, *very dour.*

'Now hear the clarinet.'

My response was instant. 'I'll play that.'

I loved the sound.

I didn't know what the instrument looked like, let alone how to create that rich tone. After washing dishes for pocket money, I took my savings to a music shop and asked for a clarinet. The salesman opened a case and out wafted a tantalising aroma of oil and wood. He did not show me how to adjust the reed or produce a first sound. At home, I took the bits out of the case, joined them together and blew — and blew — and blew. Not a single pip came out of that shiny contraption until a month later when a teacher demonstrated reed placement and embouchure.

Poor aptitude, do you think?

That negative has been turned to an asset in teaching beginners; I tell new students who struggle to break the pain threshold and produce a sound in the first lesson: 'You're ahead of me. I couldn't make a single noise for a month.'

The influence of a good teacher inspired in me a warm resonant tone and expressive scope which compensated for my incomprehension of rhythm and intonation. He gave me his undivided attention, resulting in my fast progress and decision to continue music at university.

A shy bunny from the bush, I had suffered cultural and social shock when catapulted into a large city high school. When baffled, I couldn't find the words to ask for any explanation. I sat mute when my theory teacher wrote ant–track marks on manuscript paper. I was mystified by chords called IIc–V–I or V–VI. I don't recall that Mr Teacher, a respected educator, ever demonstrated on the piano. My painful fog matched his chain–smoking haze.

I was too tongue–tied to ask for clarification.

Like a tortoise, some students scurry back into their shells at the smallest flicker of impatience from a teacher. I can vouch that some of those we consider dim may be inarticuate with shyness. Encourage them to open up with questions:

'You look puzzled; what doesn't make sense?' or

'What did that mean to you?'

If you suspect emotional issues, try: 'What keeps you awake at nights?' Or 'How's your life these days?'

Communication, maturity and experience may produce a totally different response.

In hindsight, how would I strengthen my weaknesses of aural and intonation perception? Such pupils need to sing, sing, sing, using systems like Solfa. For those with limited harmonic awareness and who are not fluent pianists, demonstrate chord progressions on the piano for an aural rather than academic experience.

✢

In the face of such handicaps, how did I struggle through to become a musician? It's a long story. But my deficiencies along the way made me a better teacher because often I wonder what I could do differently. 'How would I teach myself?'

My teaching, books and workshops are informed by a lifelong process of solving my own inadequacies. If I were to teach young Ruth, how would I improve on what well–meaning teachers doled out to me?

We teach what we needed to learn.

Part 1

TEACHER

Chapter 1

Teachers change lives

Think back to your own teachers in your formative years: those from childhood, adolescence and early adulthood. Those who fostered and nurtured a love of music so great you have continued to this time. For many young people, their half–hour lesson is the highlight of each week. The music teacher's encouragement may be the most positive — even only — adult attention they receive.

Our words and attitudes often influence and uplift lives. When a former student reminds me ten years later, 'I'll never forget how it helped when you said…' I am not only amazed but humbled by the sheer power of a few ordinary words long forgotten.

A beautiful piano teacher, Elizabeth Evans, taught me from the age of eight until 19, writes Cheryl Joyce. *She remained a lovely friend through all my growing up years and through the death of my mother at 11 years old. Thirty years later I still phone her and pick her brains for teaching tips and resources in my own piano studio. She has inspired me to care for my individual students personally and take an interest in their lives. Like her, I encourage them to try their best no matter what their ability, and often tell them they are 'wonderful'! I have several students who have gone on to be piano teachers themselves, so her legacy lives on.*

❖

Teachers are placed in a position to help the whole person — mental, emotional, physical and spiritual — not merely to drum in notes and rhythms. Those who work one–on–one or in small groups are likely to be available as a listening ear when students struggle with personal issues. How much we become involved varies according to the individual and situation. However, there will be times when a listening ear may help students cope.

Counsellors and chaplains aside, what other professionals can help people as much as the music, drama or dance teacher? They have unique opportunities to support young players on a deep level when problems surface. They can guide students into a therapeutic expression of feelings through their art. They can show them how to explore and communicate emotions where words would be either repressive or confrontational.

What teachers influenced you — for good or ill?

My opening litany of poor teaching appears to focus on negatives. Yet most of these teachers were qualified experts who just did not comprehend the gaps in my own knowledge. Or know how to fill them. There were university lecturers, for instance, who sent me to a studio to listen to recorded aural training exercises. Looking back, it was my understanding rather than my ear that was faulty; I needed clear explanation of intervallic structures and chords. A more effective approach would have been to sing Solfa in order to pitch intervals. If I could go back I would opt for training in the Kodály system.

So why, with weak musical foundations, did I persist with music at tertiary level? Literature and history had tempted me and I had attained higher matriculation grades in them. It came down to the inspiration of a teacher who captivated me with his round, warm tone and the clarinet's many–faceted ability to express moods and emotions. He listened to me — never mind that he was paid to do so! He drew out my latent ability, encouraged my playing and lifted my fragile self–esteem.

The teenage years can be torrid times of insecurity and turbulence; I typified that. He gave me hope. So did subsequent teachers. They planted creative seeds that would bud, blossom, and mature as I stumbled along through paths that ultimately proved fulfilling.

How do our students view us?

Of course not all memories of teachers are uplifting. Why did my experience of working with some experienced professionals have adverse effects? Perhaps they lacked interpersonal skills, so the developing teacher–pupil relationship stalled. Progress is often limited until the teacher builds trust. The process of trust-building requires understanding the student on various levels: developmental, emotional, familial and potential. The natural unfolding of students will be enhanced if they feel comfortable, especially in a one–on–one situation. Such trust takes time to develop and the teacher needs to understand the pupil's personality so natural reticence is not mistaken for disinterest.

Learning music leads to a special, potentially personal non-family human relationship, like something that happens with parents or grandparents, emailed American teacher, Laura P__. *The learning process, especially one-on-one, is much more personal for some students than for others. For some pupils, being open, either conversationally or expressively in music (or both) is a challenge and can impede the learning process, no matter how bright, motivated or passionate the student. This is because the student is consciously aware that their teacher's attention is fixed solely on him or her, and because in order to make music, something personal has to be given away. In these circumstances, lessons can be a challenge for both the teacher and the student. In the worst cases the teacher will mistake the student's reserve for lack of interest, though these are the students that most need one-on-one teachers and the means of musical expression in their lives.*

While it is a teacher's job to point out flaws, tone of voice and attitude can make the difference between a response and resistance. How much better if we support and encourage more often than judge! I hope none of us can be summed up in the succinct description of one piano teacher: 'Henselt kills.'

Instead, our model should be that positive thought of Claudio Arrau who expressed satisfaction in teaching, comparing it to moulding a sculpture. But he warned against slavish imitation of the teacher, pointing out that students should be encouraged to find their own ways — and themselves. (Fink, p. 260)Franz Liszt's student Amy Fay, described him as a delightful, sympathetic teacher who didn't nag but left students to their own conceptions: 'You feel so free with him and he develops the spirit of music in you... With a few words, he gives you enough to think about for the rest of your life.' (Duval, p.31)

Encourage students to think for themselves

Often we learn as much from our students as we impart to them. Yet do we give them credit for their part in this two–way, creative process? It is a process of discovery. We draw out the nuggets from reserves latent within our students and polish them into gems.

Socrates taught by asking questions. Much of teaching consists of guiding an inquiring mind. The student who analyses and thinks through problems in search of a solution will not remain dependent on us. How often do we really need to be dogmatic over technical or stylistic points? If we give students freedom to discover their voices, they are more likely to accept those instances when we do insist on essential matters.

Encourage them to develop their own sound and style by listening to others. Then, rather than becoming our clones, students can reach further than the heights we have attained. What better reference for our teaching? Have the grace to accept this as a compliment and also to acknowledge if a student grows beyond us to benefit with a higher–level expert.

In a lesson the teacher can offer the option of active participation in a two–way communication or a passive reception of directions. Far better to engage them with questions:

- What did you try to achieve?
- When you played that bar, what was the difference between now and the time before?
- What happened? What worked?
- What could you do to improve it?
- Did the tone resonate? How did it sound? What colour might it be?
- How did it feel?
- What could you do to change x?
- Was that better and why?
- What did you think about that sound? What did you do differently?
- What style, moods and ideas does the composer want us to convey?
- What is this piece about? (Many students miss the clue at the top,

words like Aria, Burlesque, Toccata or Pastorale.)
- Where is this phrase heading?
- What is the pinnacle of the movement?
- What was happening in the world when this was written?
- Where does it sit in the spectrum of cultural development, in the historical context?

How can we play music of the high Romantic era without knowing a little about the contemporary writers Goethe, Byron, Keats and Shelley who influenced the life and art of the times? What about the age of virtuosity, of Paganini and Liszt? Of developments, events, wars, revolutions? Tchaikovsky's 1812 Overture is compelling in its inspiration for he lived just after the era when Napoleon conquered the bulk of the Europe and then lost all in an ill–fated Russian campaign and siege.

Or Schumann: those delicious lyrical movements contrasted with ugly, aggressive ones were expressions of the Dr Jekyll and Mr Hyde facets of a bi–polar mood disorder or schizophrenia. Picture the Impressionist paintings while playing Debussy and imagine him sharing ideas over a bottle of absinthe with painters, dancers and writers.

Then there's the harmonic structure: what does the accompaniment do to enhance the melody line? Which part is important there? How does the key structure portray the composers' moods? This knowledge will deepen and enhance their enjoyment and motivation. With these factors, they can only improve!

Give out positives

Choose to give positive directives. People instinctively flinch from negatives like the word: 'Don't'. Far better to say, 'I would play it this way' instead of 'don't use that fingering.' Focus on what to do and how to accomplish it, rather than what *not* to do. Instructions like 'don't tense your fingers' are confusing as the brain has to unravel two concepts; firstly that of tensing the fingers, then of *not* tensing them. A simple 'let go' is more accessible. Or tell a funny story to bring a laugh.

Lighten lessons with humour

Is a serious mien really necessary if you want to be taken seriously as a 'classical' musician or teacher? Tell students funny background anecdotes and they will approach the piece with renewed enthusiasm. Composers such as Haydn wrote jokes into the music; much of Krommer and Malcolm Arnold cannot be played with a straight face. This makes lessons fun and recreational. Teachers who are able to cultivate relaxation rather than tension in their students see greater improvement, more keen interest and motivation to practice. We remember best when we have fun.

What makes a good lesson?

'Welcome students warmly to lessons and be encouraging,' writes David Shephard, formerly of Elder Conservatorium of Music, University of Adelaide. 'Convey the beauty of music and an appreciation of its moods and styles. Keep in practice to be able to demonstrate what you mean, so that the student appreciates high standards. Don't talk too much! Get students to express their own thoughts and feelings about a piece.' He recalls a student of an eminent British soloist, who said 'I learn more from my teacher by his demonstrating than by his words.'

Engage the student and they will be more likely to respond and express their own musicianship.

Chapter 2
Qualifications and skills

Write a job description for the ideal music teaching position: what qualifications and personality traits might be expected? To teach in schools, a bachelor degree from a music institution and a diploma of education is essential. A masters' degree or PhD may be required for senior positions.

The bar may be lower in home studios or in country towns where there is little competition. Skype webcam lessons may fill gaps in availability. Except when restricted by geography, music education is too important as a life–changing experience to be entrusted to less–than–qualified experts. It is inappropriate for a fourth–grade student with technical and rhythmical inadequacies to seek students—'but only beginners, of course.' In fact, beginners need the most experienced tuition so they do not formulate poor habits that will be difficult to dislodge.

Our professionalism and reputation is enhanced by appropriate qualifications. It is essential to up-date and refresh our skills with further courses and to research relevant pedagogy.

Why should studio music teachers seek training? Does it matter whether they are trained or not? Yes, very much, argues Dr Rita Crews, President of the Music Teachers' Association of New South Wales:

One doesn't need a licence to teach in the private music studio; unlike a plumber or an electrician, one can't kill anyone. Teaching music isn't a life threatening occupation; one can sit in the comfort of one's living room and count 1, 2, 3, 4 while the money magically appears.

A negative perception of instrumental teaching derives from its historical genesis as a home-based industry – even a 'hobby.' The governess who lived with the family, or someone external, taught music to the children of middle or upper class families. Before that, the employed musician within royal households often fulfilled that role. Even today, some students don't even have to leave the surrounds of their own homes to learn an instrument as many teachers do the rounds to students' homes.

The status of the studio teacher has increased as parents and students realise that teaching music is a profession. Teachers are recognised as highly trained, skilled professionals, charging fees commensurate with that education and experience.

So, who benefits from training? In the long-run, everyone does, all members of the musical trio: the teacher because training gives a solid basis for professional standing; the student because he or she is taught within a solid educational framework; and the parent because of the assurance that the teacher can be respected as an individual and a music educator who knows what he or she is doing.

There are a myriad of professional development and training courses for studio teachers, many available via the internet. Take advantage of every opportunity you can. You are a professional and should act accordingly by increasing and refreshing your skills as a respected studio teacher.

The teacher's character

Desired personality traits include endless patience, flexibility, understanding, a creative approach, contagious enthusiasm, versatility and psychological insights. Communication and people skills are essential, to apply tact in dealings with parents, colleagues and the administrative hierarchy.

Protocols must be noted and followed. In many countries it is a legal requirement that those who work with juveniles undergo a Working with Children check for criminal records and to ensure fitness to work with juveniles. If this is given the all–clear, Queensland applicants (for example) receive a 'Blue Card' valid for three years. This is a tax–deductable business expense. An example is at http://www.ccypcg.qld.gov.au/bluecard/

employees/education–and–care–services–and–similar–employment.html. Check your state or country's legislation.

Ethical behaviour and ethics are essential. There have been instances of abuse that have lasting ramifications on young lives and impact on the reputation of the teaching fraternity. Teachers must be careful in their gestures due to concerns about inappropriate touching of children. Posture, hand and finger positions all need due consideration. A gentle push on students' diaphragms was once my quick fix to improve breath support, but now I use it only with permission and when a parent is in the room.

Some teachers are concerned and overreact, judging that a consoling pat or cuddle to an upset or lonely child is risky. Use your discretion—and hope the pendulum swings back to moderation.

Chapter 3
School versus home studio

The experience of teaching differs greatly, whether it is carried out in a school or a private studio. Let us compare the two situations:

Teaching in a school

Pro:
- Provides social interaction with colleagues and hierarchy.
- Workload tends to remain regular once established.
- Facilities, resources and equipment vary but funded by the establishment.
- Teachers are usually covered by the school's public liability insurance policies.

Con:
- Organising ensembles is like putting a jigsaw puzzle together, so is scheduling lesson times around complicated timetables.
- Students may need to rotate times so they don't miss core curriculum subjects.
- Many teachers travel between several schools, each with a different system, dynamic and chain of command.

Teaching in a home studio

Pro:
- Autonomy and relative flexibility.
- Ideal for mothers with young children, saving expensive childcare costs. (Even so, it is wise to have another adult to supervise the family; otherwise you cannot give full attention to either your students or your children).
- Small children suffer less separation anxiety, hearing the parent's voice nearby. They also absorb much of the music they hear.
- Ready access for a brief 'kiss to make it better' after minor accidents.
- Proximity saves petrol outlay and time.

Con:
- Most studio clientele is after school, a time notorious for babies' crying episodes.
- It may take time to build up clientele, unlike schools where intake renews each year.
- Boundaries between work and personal life may blur or intrusions may become frequent.
- Teachers may feel lonely and insular due to less interaction with peers and other adults.
- The self-employed must ensure public safety and take out a public liability policy.

✦

Check all aspects of occupational health and safety such as slippery steps and concrete walkways, aggressive pets, obstacles. Also look to see if there are any hazards that might cause illness or harm to visitors while they are on your premises. A no-smoking policy is wise, as is keeping pets away from students. If home facilities are unsuitable, investigate hire of a local church hall or music shop. It is a bonus for the latter to offer dedicated, experienced teachers for their customers; so some set up a school. Be aware they will factor into the remuneration their space and electricity costs and that they are the ones attracting students, not you. Some teachers travel to the students' homes, in which case remuneration should reflect fuel and travel time.

How to attract students

A teacher emailed asking for advice:

A mother rang me regarding my advertisement, which she had kept. She sounded very interested to have her daughter start with me, until I nominated my fee that many teachers charge. She said that she would discuss it with her daughter and I have not heard from her since. This has happened before but I understand it is an acceptable rate. Should I lower my fees to find the students? How do other teachers get through the drought period, where there is pressure to lower the lesson prices? Should I still advertise in the local paper? I could put a notice on the window of the local butcher, where many of the local people go. I feel that mail drops cheapen me as a professional.

If people take advantage of those who undersell they are not your ideal students.

Check the recommended fees quoted on your state's Music Teachers' Association website, and adjust them if your qualifications do not match those stipulated.

Word of mouth is the best way to attract students—but beginner teachers must first find an entrée into the market. Create business cards and flyers with tear–off tabs to list your contact details. Ask permission to display them at your local supermarket, library, at record and music shops, and at local coffee shops where mothers with children gather. Carry these everywhere, even to buy milk at the corner store.

Your local scene:

- Send your résumé to the music departments of all the schools in your area.
- Pianists may offer their skills as accompanists to schools.
- Many schools allow small advertisements in their bulletins for nominal sums. Contact the school office or the parent association.
- Ditto for pre–schools if you're prepared to teach littlies.
- Offer a short recital at a school, preschool or shopping centre. Or at a retirement village with the line that it's never too late to learn music.
- Display a notice at the University of the Third Age geared for retirees with free time. Offer to give music appreciation classes and let it be

known you teach one–on–one.
- Display a professional–looking sign at a local music shop, and leave business cards.
- Befriend the music shop staff!
- Share a coffee with other teachers in the area and suggest they consider you for overflow students.

Print media:

Place classified advertisements in local newspapers, which may offer a reduced rate for weekly or monthly repeats. These are recommended as people forget, throw out the newspaper, or become sidetracked. Frequent visibility reaps best results. According to advertising gurus most people need many reminders before they act:

2% of sales are made on the first contact.
3% are made on the second contact.
5% are made on the third contact.
10% are made on the fourth contact.
80% are made on the fifth — twelfth contact.

Many local magazines prefer 'advertorial' where you write an article about an aspect of music education to be placed on the same page as your advertisement. They tend to charge for this, rather than as a contra.

Time your advertising blitz for the beginning and also the end of the school year, when there are most changes.

Digital:

The digital world has overtaken conventional promotion—and it's free.
- Google to find music teachers' directories and associations where you can submit your details, qualifications, instruments and styles as well as the standards to which you are prepared to teach.
- Post your availability and credentials on social networking sites like Facebook and Twitter.
- Write a blog to tout your educative values.

Marketing plus

Some information you might include in your marketing:
- What musical styles and levels you teach.
- Your range of students: adults, beginners or advanced: primary, secondary or tertiary.
- How long you have taught, your studies and teachers.
- List your formal qualifications and date you received them, also accreditation.
- Whether potential students might watch a lesson with a student of a similar level.
- Recommended lesson length for beginners, medium or advanced levels.
- How much practice do you expect from students of various levels?
- Do you welcome, even expect, parent involvement—for example to sit in on lessons?
- Do you prepare students for exams and if so which ones?
- What opportunities will there be to play with other students, or to perform for others?
- Do you teach improvisation?
- Do you yourself give public performances?

Maintain this blitz and have faith that soon you will scratch your head and wonder how to schedule all the influx of keen customers.

Chapter 4

Running a Business

Insurances

Private music teachers (freelance or self–employed) should be aware of the duty of care involved to run a business on their premises. You need to be covered in case of claims made against you, if you are responsible for injuries to third parties or damage to property in the course of your work. If a student should suffer an accident on your steps or be bitten by your dog, you could be sued for compensation unless covered for public liability.

Professional indemnity can cover you in the case of loss of income. Check your relevant Teachers' or Musicians' Union, or Google to find a suitable package that may include professional indemnity insurance, workers compensation (if you employ others) and personal accident insurance. Check if your household insurance policy covers using your home for a teaching studio or health and safety in a home studio.

Below are aspects to help you set up and maintain a teaching studio. It is wise to get financial and taxation advice, and to write a business plan. At least write a simple SWOT analysis (Strengths, weaknesses, opportunities, threats) to assess your position.

This website offers to organise your business with automatic lesson reminders and invoicing, track income, expenses and lesson progress. http://www.musicteachershelper.com/features–website

Money matters

Set your fees according to your qualifications and the rates recommended by your music teachers' association. A beginner teacher without qualifications should reduce fees accordingly and draw in students with lower rates. You can revise these as you gain experience.

Fees should be paid in advance or at least on the day; avoid arrears that may be hard to chase. Some teachers send out a monthly or term invoice and others accept cash on the day. In the latter case, insist on the exact amount so time is not wasted scrabbling for loose change. The advantages of the former are that students are less likely to cancel on a short–notice whim if they have already paid. Your invoice should stipulate a cancellation policy (see below). If you don't offer makeup lessons, set your rates a little lower to compensate—and ensure this is clearly stated.

Many teachers reserve the right to cancel one additional non–scheduled week off each semester, at their discretion. This covers travel and illness. However, if it turns out not to be required, the student benefits from an extra lesson that semester. Some offer a free introductory lesson to become acquainted, check standards and compatibility. Or they may suggest payment for a first lesson at that time and then allow students to decide whether they will make an ongoing commitment.

Tax deductions

Check with your accountant if these are appropriate and if so, keep receipts for:
- Purchases of music, books and resources that develop your skills as an educator, such as concert tickets, CDs, DVDs and iTunes downloads.
- Professional development conferences and seminars, including any expenses incurred in the process such as hotels, travel and food.
- Costs to maintain internet, modem and other equipment.
- Tools of the trade equipment like strings and reeds and for tuning of pianos.
- Musical instruments can be claimed as deductions and depreciation.
- Those who travel to and from private students' homes should record daily mileage in a logbook kept in the car.

- If you have a room in your house dedicated as a studio this proportion of space can be deducted for expenses such as electricity and internet costs (for example 10–15%).

Financial and tax policies differ in various countries so check with an accountant or relevant websites. The policy in Australia is:

Where an income is via institution payroll, the addition of GST (goods and services tax of 10%) may not be levied; you are an employee paid through the payroll and so are covered for workers compensation; in addition, tax is likely to be taken out.

If you are a casual teacher and don't reach the GST threshold, it is not necessary to charge this. If you invoice clients directly, GST is appropriate over a certain threshold. If you are GST–registered, refer to your accountant or tax office to check what tax deductions are valid; you will need to submit quarterly BAS statements. Private studio students accept the GST as a legal requirement.

Small business freelance teachers can choose whether to register for an ABN (Australian Business Number); it will be obligatory once your income reaches a GST turnover of $75,000 (at the time of writing). You must register for GST and you will need to acquire an ABN to do so.

You need an ABN and GST registration in order to claim GST credits for any GST you have paid on goods and services that are solely or partly intended to carry out your business. The supplier must provide a tax invoice. Businesses that are registered for GST are required to issue tax invoices that quote their ABN.

Lift your fees without losing students

How to raise your rates without loss of students? Your regular newsletter updates have told of successful performances, the high grades and wins obtained by your students in competitions and examinations. Your credentials are listed on every communication. Spell out the benefits when you notify of fee increases.

Studio fees have remained stable for the past __ years. Due to general inflation the rate for music lessons will increase from $__/month to $__/month effective from __. This will continue to include weekly private lessons *as scheduled, participation in all studio group classes, recitals and creative projects, access to the studio lending library, use of studio technology, and the opportunity to be involved in competitions. If you have trouble making the required payments for lessons, please speak to me about it, so we can work something out.*

Creative thinking can save the situation for students worth retaining. Perhaps a parent is out of work: does the student have computer or web development or graphics skills that might be put to use each week as a contra? Could the parent exchange ironing or cook a meal in lieu?

Business manager

If you find it difficult to chase tardy accounts you might team up with another teacher to phone each other's culprits. Introduce yourselves as the 'studio bursar' or business manager—a different voice delivers official clout. Or your partner may handle your business accounts in return for another trade-off.

Studio Policy and agreement

Music teachers who work in schools may be offered a contract. You can find useful questions to clarify with such employers at the websites of Music Teachers' Associations.

Those who rent space in a music shop should have a written arrangement, detailing cost of rental, notice either party must give to cancel the agreement and whether the shop makes a commission on referrals. While is not essential for home studio practitioners to issue a written statement of policies or a contract with students and parents, this enhances professionalism.

SAMPLE LESSON AGREEMENT FORM

I, _____, (teacher's name)
Address _____
Postcode _____ Phone _____ Email _____
agree to provide _____ (instrument) tuition for _____
(student's name) for 10 lessons, payable in advance, at the rate of
$ _____ per lesson of _____ minutes length plus GST (if applicable)
Total payable in advance for 10 lessons $ _____
Name _____ (of person who undertakes to pay lesson fees)
Address _____
Postcode _____ Phone _____ Email _____

Signed _____ (teacher) Date _____
Signed _____ (person who undertakes to pay lesson fees)
Date _____

It is helpful to include details of your refund, cancellation and termination policy and a paragraph to elicit background information about potential students:

Please notify of aspects in your son/daughter's development that would enable me to give optimum guidance.... Also please appraise of any medical conditions (for example epilepsy) or allergies (food, pets) and who to contact in an emergency.

Refund, cancellation and termination policy

Adapt your contract wording along these lines:

Except in the case of a student's protracted illness or extensive travel (where the teacher has been notified at least five lessons in advance) no refund will be offered for lessons missed. If the teacher cancels a lesson the teacher will arrange to make adjustments, as far as possible at a mutually convenient time. Termination of this agreement by parent or student requires a month or half term's written and paid notice. A teacher may terminate lessons due to lack of practice, poor attitude or inacceptable behaviour.

SAMPLE TEACHER–PARENT CONDITIONS

Dear _____,
Thank you for your interest in working together with music lessons.

- *Fees are $_____ for a 30 minute lesson, $ _____ for a 45 minute lesson and $_____ for 60 minutes.*
- *Payment for each month/term's lessons is due _____*
- *Families may opt to pay by direct debit banking transaction.*

My account details are _____

- *Payment is for enrolment, not attendance. Missed lessons will be charged. However, if you give me at least 24 hours advance notice, I will try to reschedule at a mutually convenient time otherwise credit from next term's account. Invoices will be sent after the first week of each term, so please let me know before then if school camps, excursions or performances require rescheduling. Make-up lessons are otherwise only offered in the case of illness when sufficient notice is given. There will be a make-up session each term that is filled on a first-come first-served basis.*
- *If you cannot attend a class, I appreciate your courtesy to inform me in advance.*
- *Please arrive before the scheduled start time of your lesson and allow five minutes before to unpack and access music and equipment. If you arrive five minutes late, your lesson will be five minutes shorter; you reserve the time slot, not the number of minutes.*
- *Students should practice regularly at home, at least five days a week. Six times is even better but you are allowed a day of rest! In busy times, a short practice session is better than none.*
- *Students will be expected to purchase a method book and other material but the teacher will endeavour to help parents budget with advance indication. Where possible, second hand music may be passed on to other students at a lower rate.*

If you have issues, please call me, email me, or speak to me during the lesson.

❖

Indicate what are your preferred means of communication: phone (and which hours are inappropriate), email or text message.

For the following version of above advice, I am indebted to Dr Rita Crews, president of the Music Teachers' Association of NSW:

STUDIO POLICY

From Notes for Private Music Teachers & Code of Ethics [2010]
The Music Teachers' Association of NSW

The following Appendices may be modified to suit each individual teacher's needs.

Standard Conditions for Private Music Tuition

- TUITION will be given by the Term of .... consecutive lessons.
- FEES for each Term are to be paid no later than the first lesson of that Term.
- HOLIDAYS:
  Lessons will be suspended during periods in the summer and on the usual public holidays as announced by the teacher; and also during any further period as to which the student gives at least four (4) week's notice that he/she will be away from home and unable to attend lessons. (In the case of a student going on holiday or leave during the term, the lessons will still be charged or the position forfeited.)
- ABSENCES due to student non-attendance will not be made up and will be charged in full unless the circumstances, in the teacher's opinion, warrant a special concession. Lessons cancelled by the teacher will be carried forward.
- PROGRESS REPORTS in the form of verbal or written communication may be provided by the teacher from time to time.
- EXAMINATIONS AND COMPETITIONS:
  The teacher will not enter the student for any examination or competition without the prior consent of all parties. The teacher's opinion as to what examinations and competitions are suitable at each stage of the student's progress must be accepted by the student.
- NOTICE to discontinue lessons must be given at least 2 week's in

advance. It is expected that students commencing an instrument will continue that tuition for a minimum of one year unless the teacher advises otherwise.

Keeping rolls

It is essential to maintain clear and up–to–date rolls, either on computer or in a book specific for your teaching. Don't rely on your memory for cancellations or changes—by the time you next send invoices it will be a blur. A double check is to clearly note at the top of each journal page the date of lessons and number within the term.

Schedules

Routine helps. The same time each week is easiest to remember and also to meet in busy lifestyles. As many students are overcommitted, give plenty of notice if you will need to rearrange lessons because of a tour or performance. Students appreciate forewarning—as much as a term in advance—if you are not available to give a lesson on a certain date. Offer several options for a catch–up lesson at a mutually convenient time, or else a credit towards the account. Accounts can then be adjusted before they are sent out or at the next term.

Offer a lesson time swap list

Some teachers offer a *lesson exchange roster* to assist with unavoidable time conflicts; for example if a student has a sporting event, doctor's appointment or birthday party. They can check the teacher's timetable, which is supplied along with the contact details of those who opt in to the exchange roster. This facilitates their ability to exchange a lesson time with another student. They should notify the teacher of changes.

All exchanges must be done parent–to–parent and not by students, unless they are adults. If two families arrive for the same lesson time because the exchange was not confirmed properly, priority will go to the normally scheduled student with no refund or rescheduling for the other student. Exchanges are reciprocal, not obligatory. Respect for privacy is essential.

Home invasions; how to set boundaries

A downside for those who teach in their homes is how to maintain privacy. The piano may be in the family living room, and thus a common thoroughfare. Offspring may troop through to the kitchen for after–school snacks. Those with young families and limited means may not be in a position to allocate a special room for teaching purposes. This may be solved if you can renovate a garage or place a demountable shed in the garden, with an *en suite* bathroom. Place chairs and a table outside so students can unpack and wait for their time—and parents can listen without intruding on your space and authority. Thus you set boundaries between work and home, so students do not infringe on your personal life. You can 'go to work' and then shut the door on it.

Notify parents of your preferred times for phone conversations so you will not be rung with the bird calls on Sunday morning, or during dedicated family time.

Newsletters and report writing

Schools will expect written reports for each student every semester and home studio clientele will appreciate it also. Many school music departments specify unity of reporting, with computerised choice of drop–down comment banks. This saves time for the head of department who checks reports for spelling, grammar and appropriate attitudes. As no two students are alike, I prefer to write according to my assessment of each player, to the chagrin of some bureaucrats.

While it is up to the private teacher to decide to write reports or not, parents do value them. A newsletter update can notify of days when changes may be made, forthcoming concerts, dates for examination entries and competition opportunities. Include information that highlights students' successes.

Time management

Schedule breaks in each session, so you have time for follow–up phone calls, bathroom visits and refreshments. If you find yourself running overtime on a particular student, discuss with the parent if the allocated time should be extended, rather than keep subsequent students waiting. Make it clear to parents that if they want to discuss an issue they are welcome to come in for the last few minutes of the lesson—not when the next student is ready to begin. Otherwise give them a convenient time when you are available for a phone call.

It helps me to set my clock a few minutes ahead to keep on time, even though I know it is so. My students are welcome to come in a few minutes early to prepare their music and instrument, so there may be some overlap. I try to place players of a similar standard side–by–side; sometimes they enjoy five minutes of each other's lesson to play some duets as motivation and enjoyment. This puts them ahead for competition duet sections and is a fun way to counter the excuse: 'I had so many assignments I didn't practise.'

('Then we will do aural tests, sight–reading and transposition.')

Some healthy rivalry may move the laggard. Watch out for off–putting competitive comments or body language that indicates this may be counter–productive.

Chapter 5

Teaching in schools and music shops

Schools vary according to budgets and the priority given to the music program—but the standard equation is that sport receives most attention and finance. Music teachers may feel disheartened that low funding equals minimal resources. They may feel isolated in a small music department, or even in a demountable building at the back behind the bins. You could build profile and relationships by barracking at school sports events in the hope that what you give out comes back to you.

Some schools employ companies to deliver one–size–fits–all teaching, with a lack of specialisation and hence average standards. Administration and peers may see 'non–core' subjects as inferior, so they are apt to infringe on lesson times for other activities. Expectations may be low and it is hard to promote the pluses to deaf ears. Even when students and parents do attend concert performances they need to be trained to sit and listen rather than chatter.

Create a culture of music in a school

Ways to boost interest in music:
- Submit articles to the school newsletter or magazine extolling the benefits of learning music (academic prowess, team–building, problem–solving, discipline, social skills). Direct them to websites that detail current scientific research.

- Organise students and or teachers to play a short piece at assembly.
- Parents love any chance to feel proud of their offspring. Encourage them to attend their concerts. It is sad that many carry and fetch their children to these but do not attend themselves. Instead they watch inferior attempts on television talent shows.
- Some teachers and syllabi offer a lower mean average of musical experiences, assuming that discussion and performance of pop and movie themes will most appeal to young players. Offer them a wide range of excellent music and you may be surprised at their tastes and choices.
- It is useful to have access to age-appropriate DVDs for stimulus and to capture imagination. Save them for special downtimes and resist the temptation to fall back on these rather than prepare lessons!

Music–focus DVD

Watch all films first to check whether they are appropriate for age groups. Some older ones may be difficult to track down and I can't vouch for all quality-wise or for their suitability. Check ratings first; I have added these where possible but they may differ in various countries. Consider editing some inspiring snippets of more adult movies, to dodge dubious footage.

- *A Coal Miner's Daughter*
- *Alice's Restaurant*
- *A Mighty Wind*
- *As it is in Heaven*
- *A Walk to Remember*
- *Amadeus*
- *Allegro non troppo*
- *Animusic* (various computer animated segments: www.animusic.com)
- *August Rush*
- *Beethoven Lives Upstairs*
- *Blues Brothers*
- *Blast! Musical*
- *Brassed Off*
- *Bugs Bunny* – segments like Rabbit of Seville

- *Callas Forever*
- *Comedian Harmonists* (1997 German biopic)
- *Counterpoint* (1968, a touring orchestra is captured by Nazis)
- *Don Giovanni* (French-Italian, 1979)
- *Diva* (French thriller, 1982)
- *Dreamgirls*
- *Drumline* (based on a true story, American high school)
- *Fantasia*
- *For Love or Country: The Arturo Sandoval Story* (2000)
- *Happy Feet*
- *High School Musical*
- *Hilary and Jackie* (Jacqueline Du Pré, through the biased perspective of her sister).
- *Jailhouse Rock*
- *Joyful Noise* (Dolly Parton and Queen Latifa)
- *Kolya*
- *Little Man Tate* (about pressures on a gifted boy)
- *Mama, I Want to Sing!*
- *Mamma Mia*
- *Mary Poppins*
- *Moulin Rouge*
- *Mr. Holland's Opus* (PG; some profanity and an inappropriate if chaste relationship with a student)
- *Muppet Show* excerpts
- *Music of the Heart*
- *New York, New York*
- *Nowhere Boy* (About John Lennon at 15)
- *Oliver*
- *Once* (Irish film about buskers)
- *Orchestra Rehearsal* (Fellini, 1978; I haven't seen it but good reviews)
- *Perfect Harmony* (G rating; boy choral musical)
- *Peter and the Wolf* (Look for the Sting version with marionettes or *Sesame Street* versions)
- *Phantom of the Opera*

- *Pitch Perfect* (has revived a craze for cup songs; http://www.youtube.com/watch?v=cmSbXsFE3l8)
- *Play School Meets the Orchestra; Play School Everybody Sings*
- *Quartet*
- *Rhapsody in Blue* (1945, fictionalized biography of George Gershwin)
- *School of Rock*
- *Shine*
- *Silly Symphonies*
- *Singing in the Rain*
- *Sister Act* 1 and 2
- *Sound of Noise* (Swedish comedy)
- *STOMP Out Loud*
- *Song of Love* (1947; about Robert and Clara Schumann)
- *Sound of Music*
- *The Broken Melody* (1938 Australian drama)
- *The Jazz Singer* (1927, then remake 1980)
- *The Music Never Stopped*
- *The Legend of 1900* (Italian, 1998)
- *The Page Turner*
- *They Shall Have Music* (footage of Jascha Heifetz)
- *Toot ,Whistle, Plunk & Boom*
- *The Glenn Miller Story* (1954)
- *This is Spinal Tap*
- *Thriller*
- *Tous le Matins du Monde* (story about a French Baroque viol player)
- *Truly, Madly, Deeply*
- *The Snowman*
- *The Story of the Weeping Camel*
- *Together with You* (Chinese, 2002, about a young violin prodigy)
- *Unfaithfully Yours*
- *The Wedding Singer*
- *The Piano (Life is a song)* Yann Tierse
- *Walk the Line*
- *Yankee Doodle Dandy*

Senior students only: use with discretion and cue to show excerpts of M and R rated movies

- *Bird* (R; depicts life of Charlie 'Bird' Parker)
- *Coco Chanel and Stravinsky* (Rated R for some strong sexuality and nudity)
- *Dreamgirls*
- *Eroica* (2003, about Beethoven)
- *Immortal Beloved* (R rating for violence and sexuality; intriguing concept lacks historical basis.)
- *I, Don Giovanni* (M)
- *I'm Not There* (About Bob Dylan)
- *La Bamba* (PG-13; based on life of Ritchie Valens)
- *Lady Sings the Blues* (R; based on life of Billie Holliday)
- *La Vie en Rose* (M; biopic of Edith Piaf)
- *Les Misérables*
- *L'Apres-midi* (adult themes but sections stand alone.)
- *Playing for Time* (female Auschwitz prisoners perform for their captors.)
- *Ray* (Rated PG-13)
- *Sweeney Todd*
- *The Band's Visit* (M)
- *The Commitments* (R)
- *The Conductor* (1980; I haven't seen this Polish film but it stars John Gielgud.)
- *The Doors* (R; based on Jim Morrison's life)
- *The Music Lovers* (M; about Tchaikovsky)
- *The Soloist* (M but appropriate for teens; some scenes of drug use. Sympathetic and realistic portrayal of a talented schizophrenic cellist.)
- *The Red Violin* (Rated R, partial nudity and sex scene but not graphic or violent.)
- *The Rose*
- *The Pianist* (Holocaust movie, tough even for adults. Strong language and violence but some scenes inspire for power of survival, music and soul.)

- *Three Colours Blue*

Documentaries
- *A Hard Day's Night*
- *Almost Angels* (1962 Disney doc about Vienna Boys' Choir)
- *A Woman is a Risky Bet; Six Orchestra Conductors* (Swedish, 1987)
- *Buena Vista Social Club*
- *Calle 54* (Latin/Cuban music features Chucho Valdez and others.) 'Wonderful performances—great for the jazz geeks.'
- *Dr Sarmast's Music School* (music education in Afghanistan), https://itunes.apple.com/au/.../dr–sarmasts–music–school/id595617114
- *JAZZ* (documentary miniseries 2001; 10 episodes)
- *Marsalis on Music*
- *Music of the Brain*
- *Spinal Tap* (Mocumentary)
- *The Mighty Uke*
- *Thundersoul*
- *The Fabulous Dorsey Brothers* from the 1930's/40's. 'Terrible plot/story but some great music including rare footage of Art Tatum in a jazz club.'
- Bill Bailey Comedy programs may be esoteric but some will appreciate.

Manage and prepare for rehearsals

Experienced teachers save time before band, orchestra and choir rehearsals with prior preparation that includes:
- Room setup; chairs, stands.
- Instruments are in good working order.
- Spare instruments are available at all times, especially a flute, clarinet, trumpet: a spare bow and a set of strings for each stringed instrument: a set of drumsticks.
- Equipment: reeds, cork grease, cleaning cloths, cigarette papers for gurgles under pads.
- A repair kit with screwdrivers, springs, oil. Learn how to fix a spring and change strings.

- Music: A spare set of all parts placed in score order so they are accessible when needed. Extra music in case students begin at the school after term starts. In allocating positions allow for attrition and absences.

Insist that students bring a 2B pencil and eraser or provide these. Thorough score preparation is essential to make the best use of rehearsal time. Adhesive fluorescent tabs can indicate cues, key and tempo changes.

Plan to begin and end the rehearsal with up-tempo energising material. Use the middle for slower paced material and to stretch them with challenges. Use positive reinforcement and vary the content to maintain attention. For optimum attention span divide the time roughly to equate to the average age of students; for example 15-year old students may wane after around 15 minutes on one activity. (Mark and Madura: p. 50)

Music library and resources

Schools vary in the amount of budget available for equipment and music. The private teacher will build up a music library over the years. This risks depletion if students forget to return loaned music or it comes back with parts missing. Note all borrowings in a book or file and the dates taken and returned. If a student borrows a solo part, reinforce by writing their name and date of loan on a coloured post-it note attached to the piano score.

It can cause disaster to school budgets if students lose band or orchestra parts. Joanne Wolfe suggests to:

Number the parts in score order then highlight or ink in the number on one of each part. This copy should never be handed out. Keep it in a separate plastic zip lock folder. This assists your end of the year sorting of music. Enlist students to sort your music in numerical order. Take the bag of master copies to performances so that if a student forgets their music they can borrow a copy for the performance only. Any music that has a red number on it must be returned to the zip lock bag.

Concerts

A soccer player does not train all season without playing a match. What are music lessons and practice without opportunities to perform? For teachers in schools, a concert may involve a military action of counting heads onto a bus to the venue, checking each student is garbed in appropriate performance uniform, herding various groups into the warm–up rooms and tuning them in time to walk onstage. Then they pick up the baton. When they have time to look back, teachers so often realise how students rose to the challenges and that this was a worthwhile exercise.

Find outlets for students to play in public, like recitals, group classes, competitions, school fêtes, festivals, and church functions. Suggest a family gathering every month where the child has an opportunity to perform a piece that they've polished. To play for grandparents who will be *so* proud and hear no flaws.

As the year ends, many students—and their teachers—are stretched, exhausted, pressured. And then comes the studio Christmas concert! (If this is the case, consider a concert mid–year.) Yet this is a high point of the year for many students, parents—and even the teachers. You may find it less stressful and more sociable to join together with a colleague and hold a united concert, especially if this means violin or woodwind timbres vary the usual piano solos.

A few simple ploys can boost spirits and increase motivation for the New Year.

My question 'What ideas do you have for simple, cost–effective end–of–year gift for students?' gained these responses:

Highlight the year's progress: 'I record my students' work progressively through the year, especially the younger students,' suggested Margaret Chalmers from Cairns. 'Using my digital keyboard's memory and storage it is easy to transfer their music to CD or DVD. I give this to them at the end of the year. They can help with cover design, for example '*Mandy's Greatest Hits.*'

Jill Kuhn from Darwin wrote: 'I have stamped some bookmarks with pictures of Beethoven and a piano and laminated them at school. They look smart and make a simple present. One year I bought some cute Christmas decorations on special and kept them for a whole year. The kids loved them.'

Studio concerts provide a supportive atmosphere, with less pressure than a competition or examination. They learn to handle mistakes in performance, to keep going whatever happens. Stage etiquette of bowing becomes natural. It's important to not pressure a first-timer to perform, but allow them to choose from a couple of easy pieces of repertoire. Even the most reluctant beginner wants to play when they see everyone else perform. Students get to know each other over festive fare afterwards and the parents can chat over a coffee. You have earned your holidays.

Tours

In the highlights and lows of touring with a school band or orchestra, surely this ranks tops of the latter experiences:

A teenage orchestra is being escorted through the security checks at the Australian Parliament House in Canberra on a lay-day when an official approaches the teacher.

'Excuse me, Sir, but do you realise that one of your students has a machete in his personal baggage?'

'*Why?*' the teacher incredulously asks the culprit, son of an army officer.

'Because, sir, in case I needed to defend myself on the trip.'

Ah, the highs and lows of touring with a group ensemble. Welcome to a roadie's perspective of touring as support act, chaperone, soloist, narrator, parent, dogsbody... What we do for love of music!

There are the fun moments of downtime, the tourist attractions—and the social interaction. The all-out highs; those standing ovations which didn't need to be milked; the packed houses playing at theme parks like Euro Disney, Lego Land, or Sea World on the Gold Coast. After the performances, the students receive their usual instructions: 'Stay in groups of four and meet at the front gate no later than 6 p.m.' And yes, they do. Musical groups tend to be reliable, disciplined and trustworthy. There are—of course!—exceptions to keep tour leaders alert. Nonetheless when a young seasoned traveler goes missing for some hours in Montmartre, Paris, he should not be surprised to be met by a riot act.

Some of my most lingering memories are of a four-state tour from Brisbane via Broken Hill and Adelaide. There was no water cooler and no toilet in the bus and often after travelling twelve hour stretches, we had to rush straight into rehearsals or performances.

Many tour members avoided the taste of strange waters in those 'foreign' cities. Looking back, we blame dehydration for much of the group's increased illness, exhaustion and loss of resilience. We now stipulate that buses have a toilet and water cooler, or else all students must bring water bottles.

By the time the busloads limped home, we were all worn–out and exhausted; a sizable number had to be taken to the doctors with flu or chicken pox; we had to wait for the trailer to be fixed. Our last concert was down to one-third strength due to illness.

We learned from this experience it is essential to recruit a parent who is a doctor or nurse for each tour. When a band or orchestral horn or bassoon player falls ill, it is a calamity. To tour a choir is far easier; SATB parts double and there is no hefting of bulky instruments and music stands.

Tours increase both the confidence and the level of performance from the players. The orchestra rises to unexpected standards; they take on tour some half–learned pieces and by the end of the tour play them brilliantly.

To organise a tour requires meticulous planning. Begin preparations well in advance, even a year before:

- Require parent permission slips, medical information and release forms and contact information.
- Enlist plenty of chaperones and give clear indications of their responsibilities and emergency contact information.
- Provide all in the touring party (students, staff and chaperones) and parents with detailed information regarding date, time and place of departure and return.
- Set out strict rules of conduct and dress code.
- Back this with close supervision, especially of curfews and unannounced visits.

Responsibility for a group of young people weighs heavily on the tour director's shoulders—and that is before he even lifts the baton! There are other cyclic swings and roundabouts: it is disheartening to farewell star senior players of crucial instruments such as horns, bassoons and oboes after brilliant final concerts, knowing that next year you must find the grace to encourage fledging players. It's important to find the internal tenacity to re-grow the program and standard; sometimes music directors might be forgiven moments of asking, 'Why? What now? How many years till we can regain the next high?' At such times it helps to pull out the files and read comments such as these from a departing year 12 student after a European tour:

'We learned not only that the European moon is upside down and that European water runs down the drain in the wrong direction: more importantly, we learned that the world is much bigger than what we see around us. We learned that other people, just like us, live all over the globe; that these people have the same hopes, dreams and desires as us; and that no matter where we are, we all worship the same God—be it in German, French or English.'

Chapter 6
Stay Fresh with Stimulus

Plan and budget ahead to attend any possible professional development opportunities for they enrich our knowledge and open eyes to new materials. They allow time to renew old friendships with like–minded professionals and to make new friendships. Other ways to refresh your skills include:
- Read teaching–related books, articles and blogs.
- Increase your repertoire of music, including styles that you don't usually play (jazz, world music, contemporary, classical).
- Meet with other music teachers to share resources and solve problems.

Teaching buddy

Team up with a like–minded colleague to share music and resources, to discuss issues and to support each other. If there is no one in your area, but you have a friend at a distance, there is still scope with regular phone calls via free Skype. Facebook and Twitter, annual or biannual conferences are good places to meet compatible friends.

Play music—for yourself

As we work with varying student abilities, there is a small but real risk we pick up bad habits from them and our musical experience may diminish to their level. Some teachers maintain a high standard by playing in professional orchestras. Others find satisfaction by joining a community orchestra or band to stay in touch with their chosen instrument, along with the repertoire, listening and ensemble skills. Those who juggle teaching timetables, their own families and running a household usually find one rehearsal a week accessible. This is a great benefit as it brings us in contact with colleagues, gives a pleasant social environment and provides the challenge of regular performances. Pianists may team up for four–hands sight–reading. At whatever level we choose, anything that refreshes and revives our love of music making is valuable.

Chapter 7
'Me Time'

Whether we work in a school or a home studio, teaching involves constant giving out—of energy, time, voice and support. We listen to people's problems as well as their etudes and sometimes take on their issues. It can feel like a one–way street. A long term can seem endless, particularly as our energy and enthusiasm wane. As the year accelerates and we crash through deadlines, we can feel worn down by students, hierarchy, administration and parents. Paperwork mounts on our desks, bureaucracy eats into the very time we want to give to the creative and interpersonal.

A stress response can cause us to feel tense, tired and to lose enthusiasm. Our usual work pressures intensify by having to be on the go 24/7. Urgent emails and texts pile up—the senders often expect a response ASAP or even yesterday. We pep up on caffeine, energy drinks, sugar and fast food, living on our adrenaline until we burn out. With little chance for downtime, we may reach empty.

I've been there, done the fieldwork and learned a few preventative measures myself! Below are some ways that have helped me. However, do check with a health practitioner (doctor, naturopath or nutritionist) for your own requirements.

When stress overloads

'I'm feeling exhausted!' a teacher posted on a bulletin board, listing her teaching load, travel, ensembles, pack and unpack, while not wanting to 'whine'. Those whose default state is to stoke up more adrenaline can reach adrenal fatigue and even suffer burnout. In this state, our immune system is so depleted that it is not surprising if we fall ill. On this hurdy–gurdy, sickness may be our only way off.

This perception of 'stop the world, I want to get off' is valid. Acknowledge it. This is your reality, not imagination. You can make proactive efforts to improve the situation, but it may be impossible to alter. What we can change is how we perceive it and how we could better respond. We can choose how we will perceive issues and how we will react. Observe:

- What's happening in my body?
- How can I release it?

We can intervene to divert a physiological response simply by the power of our thoughts. Think of someone with a similar load to you but who always smiles.

- How is this person so positive and proactive?
- How can you learn from this?

Picture a situation that has upset you. What do you experience? Observe changes to your breathing, your mind, and your body. We will find a solution for each.

On my own journey I have learned how essential it is to factor into busy schedules time to replenish and recuperate, to look after myself, to plan 'me time' on a regular basis. 'But there's no time!' It may curb the guilt to block into your calendar 'Mental Health Hour' or even better an occasional Mental Health Day.

In her book *The Artist's Way*, Julia Cameron recommends a weekly 'artist's date' when you can 'refill the well'. This is your treat that replenishes you and that you look forward to; perhaps a visit to a concert or art gallery; a walk in a pleasant park or by a beach; exercise such as yoga, Tai Chi, swimming or bike riding; a browse at the local markets; coffee with a friend; a beauty therapy, manicure or massage. If this strains the budget, consider a contra of a lesson in return for a treatment.

Below are some simple and accessible techniques, nutrients and exercises that can empower you through the three important aspects of BREATH — MIND — BODY.

Breath:

In normal healthy living, we should breathe comfortably, each breath taking perhaps three seconds rather than one. Slow inhalations are more soothing, whereas constant quick gasps may induce a feeling of unease. Studies of prisoners–of–war have shown that people who have an instinctively slower pattern of breathing, lengthening the pause between exhalation and inhalation, are more healthy and cope better with stress.

To calm, focus on slow breathing, which can include yoga–type exercises. Yogi have discovered that expanding the waistline through deep breathing relaxes the body and mind. They use deep breathing as a path to meditation, relaxation and general health.

When we are stressed, the muscles between our ribs tighten so they are constricted and cannot expand. If you inhale a long slow breath your body feels better. Slow down. Match your inhale with a long exhale.

Extend your exhale, extend your inhale, and observe how it feels. Return to natural breathing.

If your breath is steady, your mind will be also. Breathe—shrug—let go.

It intrigues me to notice in yoga sessions how my instinct is for quick inhales and long exhales–a product of decades of playing a wind instrument. Also that the necessity to snatch quick air mid-phrase means inhales tend to be taken through the mouth, rather than nostrils as is more healthy. Observe whether such habits intrude into the rest of your life. Pencil in your score opportunities to use longer rest bars to exhale then slow inhale.

- Breathe, breathe and breathe! (We do forget when we're always in a rush.)
- A weekly yoga, Pilates or Tai chi class loosens tight muscles; the focus on breathing calms and energises. Take a few minutes where possible during the day for gentle twists, full breaths or 'alternate nostril breathing' and shoulder shrugs.
- See yourself exhale tension, inhale vitality.
- Notice when your breath slows how your mind relaxes.

Mind:

Symptoms tell us all is not well with our world. What can I do to change this?

Physiological responses are linked to mental perceptions. Here are simple tools to prevent or reverse the reactions.

ACT is an acronym for Acceptance and Commitment Therapy developed by Dr Russell Harris. (http://www.actmindfully.com.au/acceptance_&_commitment_therapy). Its core message is to accept what is out of your personal control and to commit to action whatever improves and enriches your life. It encourages you to clarify your core values and use that knowledge to choose ways to change your life for the better. ACT teaches psychological skills to produce more effective management of painful thoughts and feelings. It recommends 'mindfulness' as a therapeutic intervention for everything from workplace stress to depression.

ACT breaks mindfulness skills down into three categories:
- Defusion: to distance from, and let go of, unhelpful thoughts, beliefs and memories.
- Acceptance: to make room for painful feelings and sensations, and allow them to come and go without a struggle.
- Contact with the present moment: to engage fully with your present experience, with an attitude of openness and curiosity.

Body:

Individuals are different because all constitutions vary. Some are born with weaker links and it is in these that stress brings out issues. Be aware of what is happening to your body when pressured. Look after your body: a weekly yoga class and a few minutes' practice each day eases tight muscles. Other practices you can do in a few minutes at home or in a break include:

Stretch

- At your desk, rotate ankles (relaxes the leg) and wrist (helps arm tension).
- Boost your nervous system with a spinal twist, holding the back of your chair.
- Rest forward onto a chair in front.
- Ease muscles by leaning forward onto your chair to hold your knees.
- Stand upright against a wall and lengthen your spine. Psychological

responses affect your posture, as instincts are to huddle into a protective slump or slouch.

Other ways to relax:
- Heat packs are a boon for tight muscles.
- Unwind in a warm bubble bath with added Epsom Salts (Magnesium Sulphate), which relaxes muscles, calms nerves and alkalises the system. It is helpful to ease muscle cramps. Health food shops sell a spray of Magnesium to rub into the skin for muscle relief.
- Calm with a few drops of Dr Bach's Rescue Remedy (available at health stores and many chemists.). Australian Bush Flower remedies are similar.
- My chiropractor/kinesiologist helped me in such a phase by treating the neurolymphatic pressure points at the base of the ribs on either side of the spine (known as T11 and T12). Ask a partner or friend to massage this lower back area or to gently press down for a few seconds on this point.
- Herbal teas like chamomile, Rooibos, liquorice root, or ginseng may help—and prove better than the sudden adrenaline shot that caffeine gives.
- Eat regular meals, especially a solid breakfast, or 'graze' on healthy snacks every few hours to maintain blood sugar levels.
- Schedule some time for yourself each week, and enough sleep. Where possible, curl up for an afternoon siesta/nap to recharge your batteries. Even 20 minutes gives a lift.

Nutrition:
- Check if you're low on iron (women especially) in which case some supplements may make a big difference.
- Hormone changes in women between the ages of 35–55 may affect adrenals. Check with your health practitioner.

Holistic ways to ease and resolve issues that overwhelm

Some quick–fix techniques from Brain Gym and Touch for Health include:
- Connect your fingertips together to balance and connect the two brain

hemispheres. This aids emotional centring, balance and coordination and deeper respiration. It helps release emotional stress, especially before meeting a challenge such as performance, or a confronting meeting.
- Place a hand on your forehead and breathe. When we hear bad news, what is an instinctive reaction? We hold our forehead. Similarly, if someone throws a question at us, as we say, 'I know this; it's on the tip of my tongue.' Massaging these points releases memory blocks. These are the 'positive points' or emotional stress–release points, the neurovascular balance points for the stomach meridian. Touch or gently massage lightly above each eye, halfway between the hairline and the eyebrows. People tend to hold stress in the abdomen, which causes nervous stomachs. Touching these points bring blood flow from the hypothalamus to the frontal lobes, where rational thought occurs. It relaxes your reflexes to act without thinking when under stress and to prevent excess fight/flight response, so that a new response to the situation can be learned.
- Similarly, you can ease issues with a few breaths while you place a hand to your heart.

In the same way that electrical circuits in a house can become overloaded, neurological and physiological signals can become jammed and switch off, blocking the normal flow of brain–body communication. Both Western and Eastern medical authorities recognise the need to keep the electromagnetic circuits of the body (described as 'meridians' in the Chinese system of acupuncture) flowing freely.

Applied Kinesiology

At one stage, I felt 'stuck'—that my brain had jammed up, struggling to cope with a combination of a busy lifestyle, unresolved past issues and new challenges. Sessions with my chiropractor, who practises Applied Kinesiology and Neuro Emotional Technique, were very helpful; using muscle testing, he could 'click' through various factors with the speed of a computer.

We discovered where areas of nerve interference were occurring, how they created disorganisation within my nervous system (that is, they 'switched' me off) and how to correct them. Subsequently, this technique has been used to free various tensions, many held in the body for years as the result of a negative comment or incident. I was freed from such blockages by a combination of chiropractic and nutritional adjustment, avoiding certain chemicals and preservatives, and resolving various mental and emotional issues.

Applied Kinesiology employs a holistic approach which deals with the physical, chemical, emotional and spiritual aspects of one's health. It discovers areas of nerve interference and offers solutions and appropriate treatment. These treatments cleared my mind and sharpened my focus so that I achieved far more in several months than I had managed in years before. A major plus is that AK has proved to be a form of preventive medicine, which has raised my general health by improving my immune system and helping me cope with stress.

Offload stress with a good cry or laugh

Crying releases emotions that choke us. They may include excitement as well as grief or disappointment. Accept this therapy and do not feel ashamed of tears. Another advantage is that tears wash away harmful chemicals that are produced during stressful times.

Laughter is a medicine. Smiling positively changes body chemistry and physiology. Whereas a frown increases downward jaw pressure onto the larynx, a smile uplifts with its upward muscular thrust. When we laugh, our zygomatic muscle contracts, sending increased blood to our brain. As blood pressure consequently rises and falls, the brain receives an oxygen bath similar to that from a short exercise workout.

We must never take ourselves so seriously that we cease to see the humour in situations. People have actually cured themselves of illnesses by hiring piles of funny videos and literally laughing themselves to health. YouTube clips show a long–suffering teacher confronting the Principal, a Primary Teacher and a pushy parent. Bookmark these for when you need therapy. http://www.youtube.com/watch?v=o72a_Z1fSjU&feature=related

Progressive relaxation

How do we relax? In my university days, the frequent admonishments I received to 'relax' were counter–productive and increased my barb–wire tension. Admonishing students to 'Relax!' often has the opposite effect. The words 'Let go' are more effective.

> *Let it go,*
> *Let it out,*
> *Let it all unravel;*
> *Let it free*
> *And it will be*
> *A path on which to travel.*
>
> – Michael Leunig

In the midst of a busy day, take a few moments to clench all muscles then let go.

Relaxation must be a passive, rather than busy search; the harder we try, the less we achieve true relaxation. When we go into the 'try' mode, we primarily use the left hemisphere of the brain. As the right side is more receptive, we need to integrate both sides. Meditation is one effective way of relaxing. Many find a relaxation tape helpful to focus the mind.

Meditation

Many people vouch for meditation techniques to calm their minds and focus their thoughts as well as increase concentration and enhance energy. There are various courses, books and audio productions which take the listener through stages of relaxing the muscles of the body progressively, and then continue on with mental imagery.

The Eastern tradition is to empty the mind, not only of troubles and concerns, but of all awareness. This requires considerable training and may leave it open for less productive input. Most Westerners prefer to divert attention to a specific focus, like breathing or muscular tension. Others find it easier to imagine a safe, peaceful scene.

Emotional Freedom Technique

Positive affirmations are constructive. But have you ever inwardly resisted them, feeling there is something dishonest or fake in what you are doing? Another approach allows us to express the valid reality of any situation that causes us pressure or distress—then heal the issues. Emotional Freedom Technique recommends that we voice our emotions, then place around them a frame of healing, gentle words: 'Even though I ... [make mistakes, stuff up, shake]... I love and respect and appreciate myself.'

For many of us, that's a tough call, especially if our upbringing or our peers discouraged self–love. The older generation was generally taught to be self–critical rather than kind. 'Love your neighbour as you love yourself,' Christ told us. He didn't say *instead* of loving ourselves! Some degree of positive self–esteem is essential to face and excel in performance, indeed to live a productive life.

To merely voice these words brings us closer towards solving any self–sabotage we may indulge in. Emotional Freedom Technique further empowers this process as we reinforce our words by tapping on our meridian points. This simple and accessible tool can be applied to any issue or situation and can often facilitate changes in deep–rooted attitudes, freeing us to perform to our ability. EFT founder Gary Craig describes it as an emotional version of acupuncture but without the needles. See http://www.eftuniverse.com/

EFT has been personally helpful and applied with surprising results in my workshops and coaching to help speakers and musicians who suffer jitters, shakes and dry mouth when performing in public. Particularly stunning have been the improvements with musicians, who coordinate so many aspects that can fall apart through nerves (these are not specifically EFT workshops but I incorporate the techniques amongst others).

I visited a regional conservatorium to give students a workshop, *How to Prepare for Confident Performance*, followed by a concert for students to play for parents and friends. After this I was to debrief and give further feedback and tips.

One pianist, Elizabeth, was so nervous that she stopped and started and could barely get through her Scott Joplin rag. She bolted from the piano looking shattered. I thought, 'She will probably slink home to sob on her bed in a mess of self–sabotage. I can't wait until later to give the feedback. It's a risk but I have to take this on now.' So I asked if she'd mind trying a rather 'wacky' experiment, saying I risked looking more stupid than she did, if it didn't come off—but I knew deep down it would. We tapped together while she said her version of, 'Even though I have memory blanks and stop and start and make a fool of myself...'

Then I asked her if she would play the Joplin again. She sat down at the piano and sailed through the piece note–perfect without a glitch. It was musical with rich tone and wonderful expression. The whole audience stamped and clapped wildly. My jaw dropped at the incredible difference.

The next week she played her major Year 12 exam program. Her teacher emailed me that Elizabeth tapped and affirmed before performing, then played brilliantly. She gave a 'flawless performance' of the Scott Joplin.

In subsequent workshops with teenagers, I've realised that it helps to simplify the wording for accessible, natural results. A wind player ignored my words 'totally and utterly love and appreciate myself' and substituted 'I like myself.' Her improved performance showed the words don't matter so much as long as the intention is positive!

In a workshop for teenage boys preparing their final year school music performances, a trumpeter found his own version: 'Even though I stuff up and crack notes, I still rock!' The other 16 and 17–year old boys roared approval and 'I rock' became a theme song through the whole session.

I've discovered through talking with youngsters after such workshops that those teens who observe their colleagues' improved performance gain just as much assurance for their own playing. Many of them take the techniques away and experiment in their home practice. It is a powerful learning to see and hear improvement. EFT changes lives as well as performances.

Sleep on it

Regular, adequate sleep enables us to perform to the best of our ability. People slept an average of nine–and–a–half hours in the days before electricity, technology and the Internet. These days, seven–and–a–half hours are the average, though one in a hundred manages on around five hours. Apparently, the others don't; about one–third of people in the Western world complain of chronic fatigue. This calls for solutions.

Studies have shown that lack of the important phase of sleep known as rapid eye movement (REM) diminishes our memory and absorption of information. Parents who have endured sleepless nights with young children soon realise that lack of sleep reduces their nerves to shreds, and pummels their objectivity and ability to cope with stressful situations.

I've been there. Or it's the night before a big solo or opening night, fretting, 'I can't possibly sleep!' A sedative is all too tempting, but non–pharmacological means of promoting sleep are healthier in the long run. Try these techniques instead:

The day's wind–down: Exercise in the afternoon to help the body unwind and so induce better sleep. However, don't exercise too late into the evening as it can temporarily rev you up instead. Get plenty of fresh air. It's important for good health, especially for insomniacs, who tend to breathe shallowly. Ten minutes of stretching and yoga, exercises like alternative nostril breathing, or 'meditation on a candle' will calm the mind and relax tension.

The pre–bed wind–down: Keep a regular wake–and–sleep routine. The body's circadian rhythms are disrupted unless we go to bed and rise at roughly the same time each day. If we have poor sleep one night, sleeping in only disrupts the pattern further.

Time your sleep sensibly: Where possible, try to go to bed by 10 pm to avail yourself of the circadian rhythms and a slight drop in sugar levels.

Develop eating habits that assist the body: A huge meal just before bed requires more energy for digestion and can cause vivid dreams. By eating the main meal at midday and a light evening meal, such as a salad or soup, the body, brain and digestive system are able to relax overnight. Before bed, a light snack that includes calcium, like cheese on toast, aids sleep.

Drink warm milk or herbal tea: Chamomile, valerian or passionflower before bed usually helps. Restrict fluid intake in the afternoon and evening, so you don't wake in the night to trek to the bathroot and then have difficulty recapturing sleep.

Wind down the day's tensions: Make some quiet time before heading for bed. Meditate, pray, reflect on the day's events, plan the coming activities and resolve any lingering conflicts so that they don't join you in bed. Emotional Freedom Technique can ease this, and slow deep breaths with a hand on your forehead are calming.

Release your worries: It's difficult to sleep when the day's events and aggravations race through the mind. Look at each one in turn and say to yourself, 'I release this and am now at peace.'

Water therapy: Indulge with a soak in a warm bath or spa bath. A few drops of lavender in the water are wonderfully relaxing and has been scientifically shown to increase the amount of deep sleep. Even just a footbath with hot water and bath salts will help.

Herbs, essential oils and aromatherapy: Sprinkle a few drops to luxuriously scent the bath, or release relaxing aromas in the bedroom through a vaporiser or oil burner. Of the many possibilities, the following have well-recognised benefits:
- Marjoram is said to be sedating, a muscle relaxant
- Neroli relieves stress
- Chamomile soothes an overactive mind
- Bergamot uplifts anxiety and depression; eases stress, negative thoughts and lack of confidence
- Orange uplifts and relaxes
- Lavender soothes and calms. It has been used for centuries to ease nervous states such as stage fright, insomnia, fear (of failure, of the future, of people), insecurity and panic attacks.

After your bath, lie down on a herb pillow filled with herbs such as lavender, chamomile, hops and linden blossoms. Progressively relax the muscles of your body, starting with your head and moving down. Or tense and relax each muscle group in turn.

Warm your toes: Experienced mothers know that babies sleep better, even in hot climates, if their toes are warm in socks. So, surely, do we. If body heat is not available, warmth is better enhanced by a heat pack than electric blankets, which can drain energy.

Soothe the spirit: Relax the mind with beautiful music, perhaps while reading a spiritually–uplifting book, praying or meditating.

Think beautiful thoughts: Remember that any worries and negative thoughts taken to bed with you will receive eight hours of undivided attention from your brain.

- Instead, repeat positive affirmations over and over, such as: '*I am relaxed and coping and doing fine. Tomorrow will be a fruitful and positive day. I can sleep, I feel heavy and relaxed.*'
- Write out positive thoughts and think them over and over.
- Make up short, positive 'I' statements in the present tense.
- Sing them in the shower before bed, set to your own melodies or mould them into a popular tune.
- Repeat soothing verses such as 'I will both lie down and sleep in peace; for you alone, O Lord, make me lie down in safety' (*Psalms 4: 8*); 'For he gives sleep to his beloved' (*Psalms 127: 2*); 'Those of steadfast mind you keep in peace because they trust in you.' (*Isaiah 26: 3*).
- See yourself achieving your goals, enjoying your work.
- Envision beauty.

While we are sleeping the subconscious mind continues to work on those thoughts we take to bed.

And so we wake with new vigour to face tomorrow's challenges.

PART 2
TEACHER—STUDENT

Chapter 8
First lesson, first impression

A first lesson is ripe with opportunity. Start the beginner with sound technical principles and they will build a foundation that enables them to progress faster and smoother. We know how much harder it is when we receive second–hand students riddled with faulty technique.

A keyboard lesson has an advantage over any instrument that must be unpacked from a case, with all the necessary instructions for set–up and care this entails. This procedure, and the reverse, can take ten minutes from a lesson. Add time to prepare and rosin the bow, or to wet and place a reed and the lesson is almost over. New students itch to produce a sound.

That first tone is sheer magic. String players may start with simple pizzicato; some woodwind and brass teachers prefer to begin with the student blowing the mouthpiece. Once they have crossed the pain threshold of 'can I make a sound?' they are more relaxed to focus on other matters, even if the quality of the sound was not optimum.

Psychological advantages

Even if some aspects of hand placement, fingers and posture must wait until next lesson, my goal with a beginner clarinet player is to find three notes to play a simple tune such as *Hot Cross Buns*. The student can't wait to show a parent or friend 'I can play a tune!' They are on the way, and practice is more likely.

Migrated students

The first lesson with a new student can be tricky. 'Please bring a few short pieces that demonstrate what you can do and show me where we need to work,' I tell them beforehand. 'And the books you own.' Many arrive with miscellaneous photocopies and little structured methodology.

We have to put them at ease, find out a little about their history, but it is wise to break the pain threshold early with some playing. Meanwhile our eagle eyes note pros and cons. My bugbear is that many clarinet players arrive with poor embouchures. To fix this requires several weeks' regime of 'boring' long notes and slow scales. If I send them away with a challenging piece their attention is on notes, fingerings, articulations and rhythms, anything but their chin. The student needs 'good news' to balance the fix–it. ('You produce a good tone. But we can make it even better with stable embouchure.') Or 'I hear that you play musically, now let's make it easier for you to express that.'

It is difficult to fix embouchure formation as the student cannot see what problem must be fixed. I used to set up mirrors so they could see the profile view, but now we have an easy tool in our pocket: the mobile phone's camera.

More often than not, I tell new students that we'll go back to the beginning—but move fast, so they aren't bored—'so I know what you know, and you know what I know.' Which is what I wish teachers had done with me.

Chapter 9
Choice of methodology and repertoire

In schools the choice of a beginner method book may be dictated by a band program, which allows players of all instruments to experience the thrill of music–making in an ensemble. This pragmatic choice does have downsides—the initial keys and fingerings are more challenging for some players; for example flute and oboe have less accessible starting notes and keys than does the clarinet. You may find it helpful to write out starting pages with accessible range and simple tunes that build confidence before reverting to the mean average.

    Teachers in a home studio can find methods that suit individual students and their own pedagogic principles. Keep up to date with new material. Refresh your own teaching by checking the publishers' stands at conferences or browse in music shops. While there are so many options to buy online, not all vendors allow views inside the covers. Rather than spend money on resources that may prove disappointing, team up with another teacher for a coffee, to share ideas and to look through each other's music library.

    If there is insufficient material, write your own. When I began teaching clarinet, I remembered how bamboozled I felt as a student when the main method at that time suddenly introduced the register crossing with insufficient information. I learned in a group but I was too shy to ask why the other students played higher. Memories of this bewilderment, and similar ones, meant that I would scribble exercises to help students. They became the book I wished I had started with, my method *Enjoy Playing the Clarinet*.

It takes time to get to know new students and their tastes in music. Perhaps they are not sure themselves, so try a leading question like: 'If you were given an iTunes voucher what would you download?' This can be counterproductive when you hope for *Für Elise* but they list heavy metal bands you don't know.

We hear of those educators who 'teach to exams' by giving students just four or five pieces per year from a grade book and then move onto the next level. They miss out on a wealth of uplifting music. Overfamiliarisation slumps into boredom, the student has little need to focus, and may regress in standard rather than improve. A new challenge will spark enthusiasm so I expect to offer students each week a mix of integrate — improve — polish — new material.

Here is an extreme example of how a student's standard can plummet when they become stale but escalate with a challenge:

A well–prepared student came for his last lesson before an examination. The week before, his pieces were almost flawless and he looked set for an A result. Now he sounded like another person, with errors, stumbles and wooden expression. What to do? I decided he had reached his peak and was sliding over the other side. Think fast and clamp mouth on expressions of horror and recriminations. After a fossick in the music shelves I asked. 'How do you like this Adagio?' and played a few lines' demonstration. 'Let's look through it and if you happen to feel comfortable with this Tartini, you could substitute it for the Mozart. Whichever you decide.' Keep it casual, win-win, give him the choice. Low pressure.

He understood the style, rhythm and expression from other works already played, gobbled up the notes, and it was the highlight of his performance, which gained an A+. This would be risky with less conscientious and musical students but I knew his capabilities and strengths and he grasped the stimulus with enthusiasm.

Plan and gauge material so students progress in smooth steps forward rather than in sudden leaps and regressive back pedalling. Babies need to crawl before they walk in order to master crucial learning phases of hand–eye co–ordination and brain development. So too, we must offer students well–graded methodology. We do them little service by allowing them to approximate pieces beyond their present abilities.

I wage a campaign to '*Save the Mozart*' as I often hear that poor genius massacred by students who are not ready to do him justice. The Adagio movement of the *Mozart Clarinet Concerto K622* is the most exquisite music a clarinettist will play in a lifetime. I equate it with the pianist's *Moonlight Sonata*. (Teachers of other instruments will no doubt have similar examples). We all love it, know it, long to play it. Parents boast that their child is playing the *Moonlight Sonata/Mozart Concerto*.

The simple openings of both pieces lure players in. They sail along, proud to play such a major work then turn a page to crash on the rocks of tricky rhythms or busy technical passages. Thus, early impressions of a divine work may be swamped by frustration. Perhaps teachers offered the piece to 'keep their interest' or to 'motivate them' but their initial errors and stumbles will linger in their memory. Far better to hold back until the time is right in their overall development.

If Mozart they must play, give another easier piece or transcribe it, if necessary. Motivate by saying, yes, you can play that work next term or next year, but first, let's develop tone with these exercises, legato connection with that etude, fluency with these scales.

Offer some choice in repertoire, which increases the sense of ownership in the learning. You can play snippets and themes through a book and ask them to rate each piece out of ten. Or 'I suggest these etudes to develop X and this piece Y as you play Adagios so expressively; what else would you like to learn? What styles would you like to play?' Pupils appreciate some possession of their music process, even if we must pull rank at times.

Chapter 10
Copyright and music in the public domain

When possible, use music that the student has already purchased. Photocopied materials are illegal and should not be used unless the original music is no longer in print and permission is gained from the copyright owner. A general rule is that copyright of a musical work lasts for 70 years from the end of the year in which the composer died.

Many schools have a copyright agreement such as an AMCOS licence that allows them to copy a certain amount of a work of music, as stated at www.copyright.org.au

Educational institutions have the right to copy and communicate various types of copyright material, including sheet music, for their 'educational purposes'. Whether an educational institution can copy an entire piece of music under these provisions will depend on whether or not the music is commercially available.

Most primary and secondary schools are also able to rely on a licence from AMCOS allowing them to make a limited number of copies from published musical works within the AMCOS repertoire if the purchased music is owned by the school or a member of staff. The copies must be made for the educational purposes of the school and must be marked in accordance with the requirements of the licence. Information about this

licence is contained in our publication *Copyright For Music Teachers;* otherwise contact your governing body, peak body or AMCOS.
Check with the relevant copyright council in other countries.

Photocopying has become so rife that students are accustomed to receiving copied loose pages. Parents are surprised by the concept of actually buying resources. It is a concern when many students own folders of photocopied music but not any published material. When it doesn't show the composer's name at the top all looks the same. They develop little concept of style or period.

It used to be unacceptable to perform from photocopied music in examinations but even this has been relaxed. It stretches my objectivity, professionalism and grace to examine candidates who play from photocopies of my own method, *Enjoy Playing the Clarinet*, but that is the expectation of an examiner.

Frequent photocopying means that publishers lose income and music goes out of print—and their businesses may fold. You can copy sheet music for teaching purposes if any of the following applies:

- You do not copy more than 10%. For printed sheet music the 10% rule applies to the number of pages, for electronic works it applies to the number of bars.
- You may copy the entire work if you are satisfied after reasonable investigation that the work is not commercially available (i.e. it is out of print).
- You may copy the entire work if it has never been published.

Music in the public domain can be copied if it meets the criteria to be considered as part of the public domain. All its rights must have already expired, any authors must have specifically placed their work in the public domain, and no copyrights ever existed for the work of music. You can access for legal downloads:

- **Free Sheet Music Public Domain**: http://www.sheetmusic1.com/new.great.music.html Website that offers classical works by Bach and Kohler that are downloadable.
- **The Mutopia Project**: http://www.mutopiaproject.org/ Webpage that presents free sheet music of a classical nature that people can download.

- **Public Domain and Royalty Free Music**: http://www.pdinfo.com/ URL that provides sheet music in the public domain from works created before 1922.
- **The Sheet Music Archive**: http://www.sheetmusicarchive.net/ This offers free sheet music plus subscriptions for more than 22,000 classical works.
- **Musopen**: https://musopen.org/ Website that offers access to many free classical songs and composers.
- **Free Kids Music**: http://freekidsmusic.com/ Access free music downloads of songs for learning and for fun from independent children's music artists.
- **Free Songs for Kids**: http://freesongsforkids.com/ Sponsored by *Songs for Teaching*, this music site provides free children's music (lyrics and audio), song videos, printable sheet music, and elementary classroom materials.

Chapter 11
What to cover in a lesson?

Each session should be a mix of technique and music: 'something old and something new.' The student warms up with whatever is relevant for their instrument; sustained notes for woodwind and brass students, vocal toning, scales and arpeggios. They then show the teacher the week's progress by playing the set exercises and pieces, for corrections and suggestions to improve. Some pieces will be polished in the next week. If a student leaves the lesson without some new material, I feel we have failed. Even a short, easy fun piece means they should look forward to their practice time in order to become acquainted with it.

However, to a large degree, my lessons consist of teaching students how to practice: how to gain a clear impression of a new piece or scale. They analyse, check for any 'recycled bits' of repeated material or familiarity of sequences. Before learning a new piece, they play the relevant scale to fix the sharps, flats and accidentals into their minds. It is far easier to recall a clear impression rather than to start from the beginning again.

Lessons may include sight–reading some duets to improve rhythmic, listening and reading skills. Try to include few minutes' aural training more often than not, rather than rattle the exam candidate by introducing it the week before an examination. Make a habit of finishing each lesson with a casual phrase like: 'Does all that make sense?' Or 'Any questions about today's work?' Encourage students to take ownership of their learning, so that lessons are two–way communication.

Stretch the elastic

A wise teacher knows when to let students lie fallow and when they need to be stretched out of comfort zones. When a student needs a challenge, three phrases can spark their momentum:
- What if …we played this concerto?
- Why not? (What have we to lose?)
- Do it now. Or: Just do it.

In my university days I learned this:

Weber's Clarinet Concerto in F Minor is under my fingers, I relate to the expressive shaping of phrases. Before the second round of the ABC Instrumental and Vocal Concerto Competition (now known as Young Performers Award), I perform it in a university performance practice class. All flows well. My spirits are dashed when a lecturer, John Curro says: 'Why play the Weber? Why not… Copland?'

'Because I *know* it, because I can play it well. Because I don't know the Copland Concerto and it's hard!'

As founder and conductor of the Queensland Youth Orchestra, John has seen my development across six years and performance as principal clarinet. He has rolled his eyes at my errant rhythm, but knows also my strengths. And he sees that I need a challenge. The Copland concerto is virtuosic but also allows me to express singing tone and lyricism. There are altissimo register and jazzy syncopated rhythms to conquer. And John knows that I will enjoy exploiting its introvert and extrovert qualities.

'Why not?'

'Because the next round performance is two weeks away and I have not learned, let alone played, the Copland.'

'There's nothing to lose. You can fall back on Weber. Just do it.'

How I practised. Never have I worked so hard. I had to climb a technical Mount Everest and slay dragons of my weaknesses. My rhythmic vagaries had to be drilled into precision, altissimo register runs conquered. Day and night for a month I lived, worked, slept and finally surmounted the Copland Concerto. My performance with the Queensland Symphony Orchestra was already a triumph; there was no apprehension about winning—I did so in the prior round two weeks before. This was my moment, charged with electricity.

I shone. I danced through a dazzling performance.

Whenever I notice I have become cautious in my challenges to students, I hear John's words: *Why not?* Thank you, John; I learned much from this experience.

You see things; and you say, 'Why?' But I dream things that never were; and I say, 'Why not?'

George Bernard Shaw

Chapter 12:
Practice expectations

Past generations of young people had one or two extra curriculum activities and so could focus on these. Parents nowadays attempt to give their children every possible opportunity, often stressing their budgets and schedules to do so. A big issue is the lack of time available for students to practise. With multiple after– and before–school activities, many at out–of–hours care, they rarely come home from school, relax and then practice. Or they may think it impinges on their social life. (Suggest that they hook up with a friend on Skype to play duets.)

Map out in their journals a list of days of the week and beside each write their activities. Discuss specific times across the days when they can allocate the agreed number of hours per week. Emphasise that even a short practice on a busy day is better than nothing. As a wind player, I stress that if they leave all their practice to the day before the lesson, their lips will tire and become sore. My analogy is to ask what they would think if their mother cooked a feast on Sunday and said, 'Eat as much as you can now, because I won't prepare anything until next weekend.'

Given students' hectic schedules, must teachers now accept three practices per week? Some are grateful if their students practise in the television advertisement break! An early teens lad complained that his main bugbear was friction when his mother tried to enforce the agreed twenty minutes' practice per week! A generation ago it was reasonable to expect six practices per week. The bar has sunk.

Screens rule, OK?

Rather than save time, the reality is that technology kills it. This generation is hooked into the digital world 24/7, and practice time suffers. Face to face time with friends is lost to social media, chatting online, text messages and emails. Such intrusions at all hours may limit the amount of sleep. Practice–wise, this makes a huge difference in available time compared to previous decades.

We can play the technology game ourselves, by suggesting students download various tools:

- Smartphone apps like a metronome, tuner, and audio recorder.
- Ask a student who brings the same mistakes back each week to record their practice and email it or bring on a CD or USB to lessons. Melisande liked that idea largely as her mother expressed qualms that she 'wasted a lot of time in practice' when in fact the one plus was that my policy of 'say/sing aloud and finger' had sunk in. We analysed her revealing iPod version and she went home with deeper insights to improve those entrenched errors, miscounting and unevenness.
- 'I expect my students to email me after each lesson, setting out bullet points of what they learned and how they will integrate it,' says Patricia Pollett, Associate Professor at School of Music, University of Queensland.

As technology changes at a fast pace, it is beyond the scope of this book to list all available tools. The various hardware and software is in a process of constant evolution. Indeed, the use of music notation as it has been known for centuries is being overtaken by digital audio means like *Audacity, Garageband* (for Mac systems) and *Super Dooper Music Looper* (Windows). Some appear entrenched for now: those who teach in classroom situations draw on PowerPoint and Keynote. Keyboard teachers may work with a music lab technology: electronic pianos, headphones and MIDI capabilities and software. Students can create movies and DVDs and upload to *YouTube* sharing sites. *SmartMusic* (www.smartmusic.com) and *iPas* (www.pyware.com) incorporate software to assist with student practice, accompaniment and assessment. There is instructional and note-reading software like *Interactive Musician* and the free *musictheory.net* to assist with note learning, pitch, rhythm, scales, intervals, key-signatures and sight-reading. Teachers and students can arrange and compose material with programs like *Finale, Sibelius* and cheaper entry-level programs like *Encore, PrintMusic* and *Finale Notepad*.

Youngsters ('digital natives') can enjoy the role reversal of helping teachers (usually 'digital immigrants') with the intricacies of technology (Prensky; 2006).

The many uses for such platforms was demonstrated when in 2009, the YouTube Symphony Orchestra made history as a partnership between the London Symphony and YouTube to 'create the world's first collaborative orchestra.' The whole world helped to judge digital auditions; from 3,000 videos, 200 finalists were selected. A 90-piece orchestra assembled onstage at Carnegie Hall, New York for the world premiere of *Internet Symphony no. 1–Eroica*. (Rudolph and Frankel, 2009; pp.3-6.)

Educators are encouraged to create a YouTube user account so they can access a plethora of music, DVDs, online lessons in theory, composition, vocal and instrumental tutorials (useful for those who must teach instruments beyond their training). They can create online lessons for students, show performances of pieces or post videos for a substitute teacher. Other sites are SchoolTube and TeacherTube. Like YouTube one needs to create an account, then downloads are free.

Chapter 13
Tips for the time-poor

I collect extravagant excuses like 'I had no time for practice because…the dog chewed my reed/my fingers are tired from writing so much at school/I left my instrument on the bus…' They are legion.

Apply the 80–20 rule

Many students complain of being overcommitted, with so many activities to fit into the days and weeks. Teach them to work smart and maximise results by applying the 80–20 Pareto Principle. (See http://www.gassner.co.il/pareto/)

Whether it's a scale, a technical study or a piece of music, identify where improvement is most needed—the 20% for example. (They can play the easy parts, right? So why waste time simply reinforcing them, possibly becoming stale? Concentrate on the most important 20%. Allocate 80% of time to this.)

Ask them: which 20% of work will lead to 80% success?

For example: The scale of A harmonic minor needs most work on just the top few notes. The rest is as easy as ABC. Here's the formula: 20% of the scale needs 80% of your time. 80% of results come from 20% of effort.

A harmonic minor

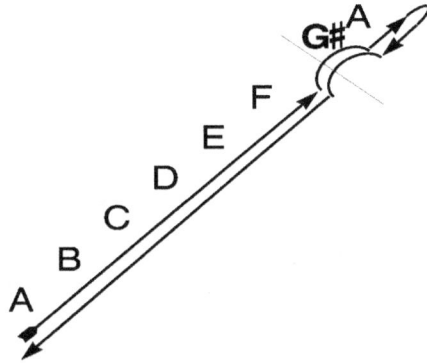

There are many more ideas to encourage practice in my book *Practice is a Dirty Word: how to clean up your act*. Here are some précis pointers:

Train the students to 'work smart' in busy times, to problem solve the most crucial bars.

- 'Practise what you can't play, instead of what you can.'
- Use available time to optimum: 'In the five minutes before dinner I'll tackle…'
- 'Practice makes permanent' so they create lasting, positive habits.
- Plan: 'How much do I hope to achieve this afternoon?'
- Stress the value of accurate, slow practice, in the early stages and for difficult passages.
- Say or sing aloud and finger before playing to form clear patterns.
- Use spare moments that might otherwise be frittered away with the many options of digital time guzzlers.

Students may appreciate hearing the honest reality of the situation: that, at times, practice will be hard and boring, that they may want to quit, or wonder why they play music. That such feelings are normal but if they are conscientious in daily practice the rewards will be satisfying.

Chapter 14
Motivate and Inspire Students

Think back to your own student days; what motivated your practice? Why did you continue? For some of us, there was the satisfaction of learning, the challenge and achievement of a performance. For others it was competition from a peer or family member, whether positive or negative. Or it may have been that there were fewer activities to compete for your attention. Perhaps that old school dragon teacher demanded the best you could give or you wanted to please the caring teacher.

Some teachers in my youth were so bad that I would hide behind a cupboard rather than go into their class, or be so much in fear of their questions that I could not stammer out a answer, thereby invoking their wrath even more, writes Sylvia Griffiths. *I also remember the other ones – the ones who encouraged and fostered the children entrusted to them – me included. I don't recall any single thing they said – the fact that these people I so admired were interested in me and noticed me as a person was enough to spur me on to greater things.*

As you get to know students, their likes and foibles, you can better offer a balance of foundation–building works and music they love—pieces that are fun to play, and give them the opportunity to express their musicianship.

Set goals: Expect the best
Students need goals to aspire to, rather than aimless wandering through a

wilderness of random pieces and the odd scale. A New Year or new term is a good time to set the pace into impetus.

With a new student or at the beginning of a semester, I ask: 'What are your goals for your music this year?' Blank look. Most aren't used to goal setting in music lessons.

My *Practice WAS a Dirty Word: Music journal* includes a page for students, teachers and parents to list their aspirations:

GOALS

SHORT e.g. Exam/recital: DATE_____	MEDIUM	LONG

Students often need prompts: What ensemble do you play in? What position? Would you like to move up the ladder? Do you have an audition coming up soon? What will you play to stun your band director? We'll need X,Y, and Z technical work, but it's do–able.

Tell me a piece of music that you really love, that you hope to play? Right, we'll put the slow movement in the Medium column, and that lively Scherzo in the long range section, say end of next year? For the Short term column, we'll map out some technical work that will prepare you for the challenges.

What about an exam? If they look horrified, this goes in *my* list of goals, to build their confidence. OK, then, how about a less threatening concert? A competition? Calm down, maybe next year. (Meanwhile, there's a book that will help you—it's called *Confident Music Performance* by Ruth Bonetti.)

It cuts both ways. Below is space for 'Mrs B's Goals.' Maybe:
- De–mystify melodic minor scales and alternative fingerings.
- Settle that unstable embouchure once and for all.

- Develop comfortable hand positions.
- Tackle vagaries of rhythm!

Both student and teacher are moving towards distinct goals, rather than meandering forward, week after week. When, mid–year, things seem to stagnate, we can look back, tick off the goals, and give ourselves a pat on the back for the progress.

Other means to motivate include:
- 'Playing music makes you brainy!' It is a simplification, but scientific studies show that music studies strengthen, even create synapses in the brain and a thicker corpus callosum.
- Through music performance we hone presentation skills that will be useful for future job interviews.
- You could support your university studies with teaching music; it earns a higher rate than work at MacDonald's!

Challenges liven and stretch, increase application. But choose carefully pieces according to players' readiness, abilities and present capabilities. If they love a piece, they understand its moods, but this does not make fingers fly faster. Hold out a bait that they can play this when they develop necessary technique by working at certain etudes and relevant scales and chords. Shun books of boring 'wallpaper' studies, whose major virtue appears to be in keeping the players out of other mischief.

Or write your own material. Many of Johann Sebastian Bach's two–part inventions were written as teaching materials for his many students. They are pleasant pieces in their own right, while offering excellent learning material.

To inspire your pupils:
- Demonstrate in lessons so students develop a concept of sound. But do not turn it into a solo or treat it as an opportunity to practise for tomorrow's concert.
- Play duets together.
- When a student has conquered a work, record them. There is good quality equipment on most computers, or invest in a sound or DVD recorder. Save the file to send home on mp3 or disc.
- Play recordings or steer them towards top performers on YouTube. (There are many of a dubious standard.)

This quotation from Goethe resonates in my mind with excellent results: 'Treat people as if they were what they should be and you help them to become what they are capable of being.' If we expect good results, we are rarely disappointed.

Stickers

A common motivation is to give out stickers, especially for the very young and for beginners. One can make a point with the judicial choice of a sticker comment, and whether it is a mere star or a 'Wow!'

Are they overrated? A sticker thief showed me just how much stickers are prized. A student's eight-year old brother often sat in the room with their mother. As I accompanied on the piano he would sneak to the table and choose his unearned booty – until banished from lessons.

When teaching adults I ask, 'Are you too old for a sticker?' and they always laugh and shake their heads. I often forget to give stickers to older students who are consistent and conscientious, for this is their norm. When I do remember they gratefully accept. A discussion with teenage students elicited the information that ordinary stickers didn't cut it, but they love scratch-n-sniff, puffy, scented, sparkly diamantes and furry gimmick ones. A quick Google for sticker suppliers shows a wide range of styles, including customised ones that include your own name and comments like 'Ms Blogs says you're a star.'

Teachers have various systems of sticker charts and offer prizes after students attain filled columns. Each weekly page of my practice journal *Music WAS a Dirty Word* includes five stars so the teacher can decide how many to highlight.

We can vary the principle by drawing a star in pencil next to a piece. Next week when it shows polish, add a gold or silver adhesive version. Sometimes I ask a student to assess their playing of the work out of ten, which is written under the date. The following weeks we again rate it and they enjoy satisfaction as the number rises.

Chapter 15
Understand Development Stages

Ages and stages

Students pass though valleys and slumps before moving to each mountain vista. These are useful for developmental learning as long as people do not stay there beyond each usual phase. It helps to think where they are on their journey through life and how this affects their responses.

For the toddler life is exploration, discovery, ripe with opportunity. They are open to all options and life is all play. The youngster begins to realise that practice, even scales, are expected. That they may be dressed up in a bow tie and cummerbund and expected to perform.

The teenage years are most difficult as students face conflicting issues, including the intrusion of hormones and relationships. Music is not cool, unless they have access to a guitar or drum kit. If as a teacher or parent you decide to embrace this rite of passage, allow them the garage for rock band practice, the digital keyboard to compose, arrange and record their songs. They will retain a love of music even if it is not a style we might wish. As a mother of sons, I can vouch for the value of rock bands: if it helps a boy retain his self–esteem through these fragile years, he will come through.

The next phase is university, when students show eventual maturity and self–direction. There will be pressure of assignments as before but they increase in ability to plan and meet deadlines.

Childhood cognitive development passes through four distinct phases according to the 'Stage Theory' of Jean Piaget (1896-1980):
1. **Sensorimotor Stage** (birth to age 2) Pre-language; learning through the senses and through motor interactions with the environment. Infants learn through trial and error, rely on instincts and modify them to adapt to their world.
2. **Preoperational Stage** (ages 2–7) Language development; ability to imagine unseen objects; symbols take on meanings; learning through the senses. As with the former stage, they are egocentric. They tend to focus on one aspect or dimension of a problem. Understanding is perception bound, in the present.
3. **Concrete Operational Stage** (ages 7–11) Ability to understand concepts of timbre, tempo, duration, pitch and harmony; ability to use deductive reasoning; ability to understand the world from others' perspective.
4. **Formal Operational Stage** (approximately ages 11–16) Can think logically, abstractly; can find multiple solutions to problems; Can understand musical notation. (Piaget; 1963)

Milestones of musical development may vary but a general guide is as follows:

Birth to ages 2-4: Absorbs and unconsciously collects sounds in the environment; moves and babbles in response to these sounds.

Ages 2–4 to ages 3–5: Imitates simple tonal and rhythm patterns of music in the environment; can hear different pitch levels.

Ages 3–5 to ages 4–6: Can hear differences in dynamic levels; can perform simple rhythmic and tonal patterns; can coordinate singing, breathing and moving.

Ages 6–7: Can hear differences in tempi; vocal intonation begins to stabilise.

Ages 7–8: Can hear differences in timbres as well as consonant and dissonant sounds.

Ages 8–9: Rhythmic performance begins to stabilise.

Ages 9–10: Can hear and perform simple harmonies; melodic performance begins to stabilise.

Ages 10–11: Harmonic ability begins to stabilise. (Mark & Madura, 2010, p. 76)

Family situations/ position in family/sibling rivalry

Psychologists consider that birth order plays a part in shaping development and personality.

- Eldest child: These have been 'crown prince' or 'princess', privy to family secrets—until supplanted by the next child. They may need to retain supremacy over later siblings by suppression or industrious work, so they tend to be conscientious and anxious to please. They have had more quality time with parents so relate well to adults. A string player may be an eldest child as he or she is used to perseverance reinforced by parental interest. They may be leaders, hard–working and successful.
- Middle child: These have not had their parents' undivided attention and can feel squeezed after another child is born. They try to catch up on the older sibling. They will probably choose opposite actions and activities, just to be different. If they feel displaced in a family they may develop problem child tendencies. Often they are adaptable and independent, with the mantra 'I can work it out.'
- Youngest child: May feel powerless, as others are older and bigger, more capable. Will either feel inferior or speed to overtake brothers or sisters. As parents have loosened control, constrictions are relaxed; life is a party, fun and relaxed; older siblings have blazed the family trails so younger children may follow in their steps quicker and easier. They may be attention–seekers, as they must compete with the siblings.

When progress slows, take heart that it's not always about us. A half-hour music lesson constitutes 0.3% of a student's week. They live most of life away from us and for some this is a jungle. They may be distracted from their usual diligence by distressing home issues. Parents fight or separate or divorce. Multi–strand families require adjustments to overcome frictions with step–parents or new siblings. Perhaps they are bullied at school or on the internet. They may welcome opportunities to offload such troubles to an objective ear.

Let us not judge students hastily. If their issues emerge, we may become more understanding. The delightful French documentary film *To Have And To Be* tells of a one-teacher school in a small rural district. The teacher's ability to quietly support students, to challenge them and draw the best out of them shows just how a positive influence enriches young peoples' lives.

Adult students

Mature aged students should be dreams to teach; they are motivated, attend because they want to and not because a parent dictates that they learn. For some, to learn music is the fulfilment of a lifetime longing. Some—not all—have time for diligent practice. Others feel guilty because their great expectations of regular practice are stymied by the need to fit it around work hours and pressures. Many derive satisfaction from joining beginner bands with others of similar standards.

They are self-aware—often too much so. But it does appear that adults have a premium on self-sabotage. Many assume that youngsters play better, blessed with youth's life force. They forget that many adolescents lack motivation, time-management and discipline and that they may approach music as one activity amongst many.

The mature aged learner has one significant disadvantage; their parents skimped on praise. In that era, accolades were rare because to 'get a swollen head' rated just below diphtheria or polio. They may have been told to sit down and 'be seen but not heard.' Recent generations of young fry are applauded for every modest attempt, their parents reinforce and validate at every turn; their painting daubs adorn the refrigerator. As a result they are confident and capable—if they will only maintain practice in over-busy schedules. Adults need constant encouragement especially if they challenge themselves with an examination, competition or recital.

Kind words can be short and easy to speak, but their echoes are truly endless.
— Mother Theresa

Rites of passage

You know those holding patterns when planes circle the sky, waiting for space to land because fog in another capital has wrought havoc on schedules?

Time in the ceiling on recent flights clarified for me some mid–teen students' issues. They spend months or years in holding mode, distracted by hormones, technology and social media. Yet if we can maintain their interest long enough, they come through the fog and land a stunning performance.

It can be disheartening when last year's model student becomes scatty and only interested in the opposite sex. Experienced teachers know well the trials of seesaw mid–teen years. Tell yourself that most will emerge like butterflies from their chrysalis. Even though the transition to high school is a crucial drop–off time, those stayers become mature and sensible.

Another rite of passage comes when a student announces: 'I can't continue as I'm going to the orthodontist to get braces.' This is most distressing for woodwind and brass players. They can be reassured that many others have survived this without curbing their music; there may be occasional times when the braces were tightened but an analgesic eases pain. They may cover the teeth with mouth guard or a piece of florist tape.

Final year students are stretched and overcommitted. Suggest that they maintain music as downtime, and see it as recreation and a highlight of the week, rather than yet another guilt trip. Then they may last the distance. We do need to be aware when there are valid reasons why practice has been minimal, especially with senior students. Or why they can't meet all commitments.

Band director: 'If you miss rehearsal next Sunday, you're out of the band program.'

Student: 'Sunday is full tilt already with the soccer game and drama dress rehearsal.'

Director: 'That's the bottom line; you come or you're out.'

Exit one talented, musical player who will jam and compose on drums and piano, but rather misses his trumpet.

When my students didn't practice, I was a typical monster–teacher. Earlier. Until I suffered with my own sons through upper high school mid–year crises—like Year 12 Music and Drama Extension assessments.

Scenario 1: the Ancient Moi:

'What, no practice again? Assessments, two oral presentations, exams, you say? Sniff. Well, it's against my principles to take your parents' money for zilch improvement. Remember, I have a waiting list... Oh dear, have a tissue. Cheer up, of course you *can* play well. With a bit more practice. I mean, lots more. C'mon, wipe your nose and let's try it again.'

Not surprising that they decide to put their time into gaining higher matriculation results.

Scenario 2: the Nouvelle Moi:

'Had another tough week? Hmm. Let's do some Aural Tests. (Groan) OK, we'll hear some terrific, really inspiring recordings, play sight–reading duets. I'll tell you some General Knowledge stories about musicians' lives and hard times—depressive ones like Schumann.'

You may call me a softie but I lost fewer students with Scenario 2; they enjoyed their music as a ray of light in otherwise dark weeks. Some reappeared years later, and spent whole lessons conquering the scales they couldn't face back in high school.

Believe in the long–term processes of your teaching. Freed from guilt–trips, students can better express their musicianship and ability. If they enjoy their music as one haven in their stressful lives, they can go on to shine.

My best tactic to motivate is to analyse students' temperament in order to best relate to them.

Chapter 16
Understand People to Motivate

The 4 Temperaments

All students are different and so our approach to each will vary. Do you struggle with a student who doesn't respond for all your efforts? Perhaps it would help to understand according to the temperaments, a concept that is as old as Hippocrates and was popular in Shakespeare's day as the 'four humours'. I find these clearer than the Myers Briggs' system. People do not fit into neat categories, but most have a strong leaning towards one or two of the following:

SANGUINE Extrovert, talker, 'natural' performer, pleasure seeker, sociable. Over–committed, so often late. Praise helps them to keep going. (Tigger)
MELANCHOLIC Introvert, thinker, perfectionist, pessimist, sensitive. Give sincere, supportive praise; encourage towards goals. (Eeyore)
CHOLERIC Extrovert, leader, doer, optimist, ambitious, task–oriented, hot–tempered. Ease workaholic trait, be tolerant of others in groups. (Rabbit)

> **PHLEGMATIC**
> Introvert, quiet, mediator, watcher, pessimist, steady, resists change. Help to set and achieve goals, make decisions, accept responsibilities. (Winnie the Pooh)

Sanguines are the bright chatterboxes who natter in rehearsals. They welcome performance and thrive onstage as they love attention. Their enjoyment means nerves less affect them. Their enthusiasm is infectious, so they inspire others to join ensembles and bring friends along. The downside is that, having agreed to an examination, they baulk at scale practice, as it is boring and routine. They prefer to have fun rather than process dull routines. Their attention span is based on whether or not they are interested in the person or event. The Sanguine can change their focus or interest in an instant. Sanguines are competitive and tend to be disorganised. Unless very disciplined, the Sanguine will have difficulty controlling their emotions. As Sanguines take on too much, they spread themselves thin and have problems finishing tasks. They need praise like oxygen, so find, and even invent a positive word to help them along.

A Sanguine parent may talk through concerts and may attempt to tell the story of their lives, as you are about to pick up baton to rehearse. After a band concert or tour they arrive last to pick up their child because they are over–committed.

Melancholics are perfectionists, so they expect high standards of themselves and others. They are creative, inventive and artistic; music allows them to express deep feelings. They can be genius–prone, deep thinkers, and prove innovative musicians—if their perfectionism doesn't get to them. Be careful with criticism, as they are prone to depression. They are so sensitive that they have filed away every negative word from way back. They need encouraging praise but it must be sincere and honest or they see through it; even so, they tick through, asking why did she say that? Melancholics can't just accept and enjoy. They are conscientious, so will work hard if engaged. As they thrive on process–type activities, they may not baulk at scales practice. Help them to not put unrealistic standards on themselves and others. They may fall into analysis paralysis or tangle themselves in loops. Encourage them to meet goals.

Melancholic parents may expect perfection, worrying that their child won't meet the exam standard.

The **Choleric** loves to be in charge so is often a leader of an ensemble. Tells people what to do, is decisive, able to motivate, knows what is right. Has trouble accepting other points of view, doesn't always listen and can be outspoken so may alienate others. Often is a visionary and seems full of practical ideas, plans and goals. The Choleric does not require as much sleep as the other temperaments so their activity seems endless. They are purpose–driven and results–oriented and tend toward the obsessive workaholic. They are an asset in that they take on responsibilities; they may be there early to put out music stands. They need to take the pressure off others.

A Choleric parent may take time from rehearsal by arriving five minutes before and attempting a takeover of the director's authority. May tend to dictate the position and how it must be for the child.

Phlegmatics are introverted and don't like to be pushed out of a comfort zone. They hate a change of status quo or having to fix problems. Routines can appeal if they are given a chart to tick off items like scales. A Phlegmatic is the easiest temperament with which to get along. They live a quiet, routine life, free of the normal anxieties and stresses of the other temperaments. Phlegmatics may avoid getting too involved with people and life in general, but their steady personality makes them an asset to ensembles. Phlegmatics seldom exert themselves with others or push their way forward but let things happen. We teachers may find them steady and reliable. Except when we thought they agreed to do an exam; they don't like to offend, so are reluctant to say no. Instead they vote with their feet or fingers and don't prepare. 'I thought we were going to do this exam' could meet with '*You* thought but I didn't'—except they will think rather than say it. They find it difficult to accept responsibility or commitments, so they procrastinate and hope the issue will go away. If they must change an aspect of technique, give reasons and stress the benefits. If they think it is worthwhile, they may give it a chance. Offer time frames and make sure they agree. Give them the opportunity to say no.

The Phlegmatic parent just wants offspring to have fun, but not be stretched beyond their comfort zones.

Let us apply this to a string quartet. Perhaps the Choleric leader is abrasive and upsets the Melancholic cellist or the second violinist Sanguine, so the peacemaker Phlegmatic violist may pour balm on choppy waters.

Websites offer questionnaires to discover predominant temperaments. None of us fit into neat boxes; just as we are all a mix of positives and negatives so we may be a combination of several temperaments, or change as we mature and learn through life. However it is helpful to understand students and change our approach, if it has been counterproductive.

To apply this, think of your problem students:

Student name	Issues	Temperament(s)	Actions
_____	_____	_____	_____
_____	_____	_____	_____
_____	_____	_____	_____
_____	_____	_____	_____

A similar system of analysis is the Enneagram, which measures personality along nine different scales.

Apply the five love languages

When students are unresponsive, it may help to analyse our actions to see if we are using the approach that may best click with them. People tend to relate through one or other of five 'love languages' according to Gary Chapman, author of *Five Love Languages* (Northfield Press).

Consider that problem student. Which of these aspects appears to gain best interaction?

Words of affirmation: For this person, unsolicited compliments have great impact. Insults are distressing and hard to shake off. They flourish when told: 'You did great!' or 'I value your effort' or you express some other kind of appreciation.

Quality time: Undivided attention makes this student feel valued and appreciated. A student who was diffident in a class situation may blossom one–on–one. Distractions and a failure to listen can be hurtful, so music lessons can mean a lot to such people.

Receiving gifts: This student will warm to a well–chosen reward for good work. Be lavish with sticker awards, certificates or chocolate, if appropriate.

Acts of service: This person feels loved and special when people do something practical for them, as they tend to do for others. They may ask you for help; they love to do things for others but if they don't feel served in return may feel neglected.

Physical touch: These people crave physical touch, the hugs, cuddles and the reassurance of contact. This is a difficult one in a society that asks us to curb our natural instinct to pat students on the shoulder when they are upset. Some children spend long hours away from parents; before– and after–school care can add up to twelve–hour days away from home. Use your discretion.

Chapter 17

Crowd Control for Group Teaching

Much of this book focuses on the private studio, as school situations differ so greatly. However, many teachers will need tactics to manage a group of skittish children who vie for attention. How to give individual attention to each, while keeping the others occupied so they don't chatter or sword fight and poke out eyes with the violin bows? If our voices compete with loud squawks they may suffer strain.

Keep them busy

There are a wealth of downloadable puzzles, theory sheets, composition tasks and quizzes at sites such as http://www.musicfun.com.au/

- Be aware of progress and draft the fast moving students from the slower ones.
- Harness competition. This works a treat with some students but is anathema to others. Use it with discretion.
- Use duets, trios and quartets as much as possible.
- Adjust your expectations, as group progress may be slower than one–on–one. But keep an open mind. I have recommended clarinet beginners start at age 11 or 12 for maturity and physical size and when teeth settle. My reservations about teaching Year 4 beginner groups have been proved wrong. Most of these children learn fast and gobble up the carrot of a simplified *Pink Panther* supplementary to their band

method. Each new year's intake is rearing to play this; once it was a highlight of fourth term, but now some manage it much earlier.
- Open their ears by demonstrating snippets of flashy music, and expressive tone; steer them to find more on YouTube. Year 4 students were intrigued when I played an altissimo note to shush them (rather than strain my voice). As they were fascinated by the wall fingering chart, I decided there was nothing to lose and taught them top notes—in their first year of learning. This was a lesson for me as well; don't underestimate what can be achieved in a group beginner lesson.
- We scramble to listen, write comments and what to play on the sheet for all group students. Instead I prepare a small notebook for each, with space for each week. Each now writes three points to remember and what pieces they should work on.
- When a student is frustrated by the pace of the mean average, suggest a once–off individual lesson to spark them, or that they move to one-on–one lessons.
- While each student plays a piece, others might 'accompany' with less noisy percussion instruments like maracas or triangle.
- Students can be encouraged to listen to others and give supportive feedback. Curb derogatory comments.

Chapter 18
Rhythm repairs

Teacher: *That note is too short.*
Student plays.
Teacher: *Now the note is too long.*
Student thinks: *I'll fix you.* Student plays.
Teacher: *The note is too short.*

Many players try to manage on 'hit and miss' or 'near enough' counting, or no counting at all—as I did in my teens. They fool themselves if they imagine this is not obvious to a discerning listener. An adjudicator or examiner can usually tell in the first line which candidates do not have a reliable system of counting.

It starts at the beginning. School band programs are under pressure to produce a lively performance after a short time, perhaps for the grandparents' day. Something showy, jazzy and bright, please. That means syncopated rhythms and tied notes from those who struggle with ta ta titi straight beats. The quick fix solution for the band director is to sing, play or whistle the rhythm so students can copy. They thus miss an important foundation of understanding the structure of beats and note values.

Just 'counting' is not the issue. Accurate, reliable rhythm is not just a matter of saying or thinking '1–2–3–4' (perhaps uneven, perhaps not). The foot–tapping method is fallible. A heavy thumping boot doesn't ensure even measures, as that foot may slow to fit a string of notes into the beat.

In past generations, children lined up for assembly then marched into their classrooms. This imprinted a strong sense of rhythmic pulse and also the cross–crawl movement activated whole brain learning. Studies show that physical movement helps our brains absorb information better. Cross–crawl, or cross–lateral walking in place, involves alternately moving one arm and the opposite leg and then the other arm and leg, such as when we march. This accesses both brain hemispheres simultaneously and is an ideal warm–up to improve coordination, breathing and stamina, and to enhance hearing, vision and learning.

Pupils who have little sense of pulse benefit from movement; in Germany I taught a lad who had sketchy rhythmic sense. We paced the school corridors intoning *ein, zwei, drei, vier* which helped him process time values. Ask students to walk a tempo, with longer or shorter strides, or different notes, or to hold a foot for the length of each note, 1–2–3–4. (This enhances spatial awareness.) Or they can walk while clapping the difference between duple, triple and quadruple. Suggest if the student has a dog, they take it and their music for a walk and sing their piece through.

The Dalcroze system includes kinesthetic rhythmic movement called Eurhythmics. The premise is that rhythm is the primary element of music and that the natural rhythms of the body act as the source of any musical rhythmic experience. Daniel Baxter, Brisbane teacher and counsellor, shares his rhythmic experiences from primary school through to university:

I always struggled to know where the pulse was and how the rhythm fitted in with it. I relied upon people to work out the rhythm for me, or to follow a stronger player in an ensemble so I could then memorise it. When I got to university, I could no longer rely on the help of others, particularly with rhythm dictation in my aural classes.

My fantastic lecturer for aural studies gave me extra sessions to improve my rhythmic dictation. However I still struggled, until I began doing Dalcroze Eurhythmics, which took rhythm from being a set of notes on a page to being a living, breathing thing – as rhythm actually is.

I was able to feel the space that certain notes took up; what a crotchet or a quaver felt like and in a very real sense, see how it fitted into a tempo. Walking a beat, whether a crotchet, quaver, minim or a semibreve, gave me a whole other view of how rhythm works. I am a strong believer in the fact that music is a felt thing, not cerebral. For music to be experienced, it must engage not just our ears but also our emotions, our minds and our bodies. This has benefitted me, and it benefits the students that I teach.

Students may replicate our demonstration during the lesson but forget it by the next practice. Turn technology to good use and record the correct version on their mobile phone or email it to take them through the week.

Pupils also hate it when teachers ask them to clap, though that's actually another quick fix to improve confusions and irregularity. Invest in a few percussion instruments like bongo drums, triangle and maracas, or—less cool—they can put together a home drum kit with saucepans and empty upended ice–cream containers. My students love to let loose on my son's drum kit.

Students must understand the relationships of rhythm values, and how they subdivide. Many are left cold by diagrams that show a tree of notes. The ever–increasing number of tails can bewilder them, as can meaningless names like quaver and crotchet.

The logical system is the Germanic–American one where whole notes are divided into half notes, quarter notes, sixteenth notes, thirty–second notes and so on. All children understand money:

A whole note= $4= 4 x $1= 2 x $2= 8 x 50¢= 16 x 25¢
A half note= $2= 2 x $1= 4 x 50¢= 8 x 25¢
A quarter note= $1= 2 x 50¢= 4 x 25¢
An eighth note= 50¢= 2 x 25¢
A sixteenth note= 25¢

Every beat matters in music. Impatient students hate to wait on longer notes and think it doesn't matter if they cut them short. Even a missing sixteenth note will throw the music out of synch. Missed beats are like being short–changed in a shop. So it is not unreasonable that students who make a habit of shortening the time values could be fined for each beat they miss, to be donated to the charity of their choice.

- **Subdivide**: Once the basic rhythmic values are clear, subdivide to the lowest common denominator. Choose a small unit for counting. If eighth notes predominate choose these as your currency. Smaller black notes (sixteenths, thirty–secondths) seem less threatening when slotted into frequent beats rather than fit a mass of notes into one long, bigger beat.

Whiteout: A student's brain may spasm at the sight of thick–tailed sixteenths and thirty–secondths notes. Pieces which bristle with thick–tailed sixteenths, thirty–secondths notes or worse, like the snippet from Debussy's *Petite Piéce*, can be clarified by eliminating one set of tails— sixteenth notes are now eighths, quarter notes become half notes and so on. You can do this with any difficult piece of music. Either write out a phrase, omitting one set of tails, or photocopy the section of your music and use whiteout to erase tails from notes. I use small white adhesive labels or tear off border bits from merit sticker sheets. This avoids the chemical smell and affect of whiteout. A threatening mass of tails becomes clearer and easier to decipher.

- **Mental Automatic Ticker**: Suggest students imagine a metronome inside their heads. They tick continuous subdivided beats to make sense of length and subdivisions.
- **Audible Ticker**: The student plays each subdivision by re–articulating a regular pulse through long notes. When this snippet of *When the Saints Go Marching In* is re–articulated the length of long notes becomes clear.

- **Catchwords**: An intuitive way to learn is to draw on the natural rhythms of language. Make up words to go with the patterns: for example:
  App–le or man–go for quavers
  Croc–o–dile or pine–app–le for triplets
  Ams–ter–dam or kang–a–roo for dotted triplets
  Cat–er–pill–ar or Co–co–Co–la or wa–ter–mel–on for sixteenths

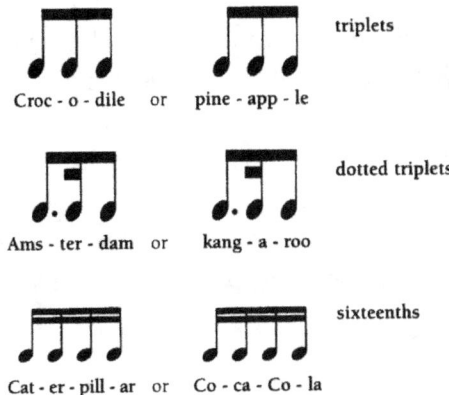

- Students say aloud or sing in the rhythm while they finger the notes.
- They can play just the rhythm on one repeated note or on bongo drums rather than coordinate notes and rhythm at the same time.
- **Demystify syncopations**: These make sense if students take out the ties and re–articulate their notes. I add white adhesive paper from the sticker sheets then remove it when the rhythm settles.
- Pencil strokes: A sight–reading quick–fix (especially useful with long bewildering passages of notes) is to take a few moments to pencil above the notes where the beats should fall.
- **There is no dogmatic 'best' way**. Students might choose a combination of several systems: sometimes thinking 'ta ta ti ti tiki tiki ta', sometimes counting numbers. They might even choose to fiddle with the 'correct' counting, for example thinking 1 2 3 4 5 on the long, tied notes in *When the Saints Go Marching In*, instead of 1 2 3 4 1 as it should be. (Above) Who's to argue if it comes out correctly and clearly? Listeners can't hear what is happening inside their heads.

The main thing is that students mentally tick through regular beats. They can choose whichever system works well for them. Another way to improve rhythm is to put one–on–one students together as a duo or overlap five minutes of two pupils' lessons so they can play duets. (When I play with them, sheer habit makes me accommodate poor counting.) Or suggest they tape one line of a duet and play along with it. If they don't play in time, any correct note in the wrong place is a mistake, just as a weed is a plant growing where it shouldn't. Sight reading with friends or playing in an ensemble helps students to develop the useful skill of keeping going when lost, listening and jumping to the correct bar.

Asked to help students flummoxed by their tricky marching band rhythms, my first step was to enlarge their music to A3 size –for practice purposes. It's hard to face music that's barely legible. Step two was to simplify complex rhythms. When I blanked out syncopation ties and a whole set of rhythmic tails they made sense.

Reading Rhythms

'Most music students need to significantly improve on reading rhythms, more than any other aspect of what's written', writes Tom Beek, lecturer at Fontys Conservatory in Tilburg Holland. 'To build their confidence, I practise reading rhythms with them, apart from the sight–reading on their instrument. This goes from simple (clapping the rhythm while saying 1–2–3–4) to complex (sing the phrase while tapping on 1 and 3.) These two ways fit most with jazz and pop–related stuff. Dancing and sports also can widen the rhythmic consciousness of a student. One of my students improved dramatically by singing and improvising while he was jogging. This confirms my concept of rhythm consciousness as something very basic, physical, non–verbal, more body than mind related.'

Chapter 19
Note reading

Music is a language. However many beginner students resist learning to read. Children of musicians have acute aural perception and some find playing by ear or memory easier than learning note names. How many times must we explain FACE for spaces and 'every good boy deserves funparks' (my students prefer 'empty garbage before Dad freaks')? We bring out the flash cards and give jellybeans for correct answers. And then they still want to pencil the notes underneath, sometimes incorrectly. One day it all clicks and they're away.

Introduce a student to a new piece

Help your student begin a new piece to form a clear impression. Even sight-readable, simple pieces benefit from a clear first reading. It is far easier to pull out weeds (or wrong notes) when they are spindly, before they grow tough trunks. Create in students the habit of 'play it right' rather than of 'play it wrong', otherwise known as hit'n'miss.

- Away from their instrument, pupils begin by looking through new music as if reading a book. Note issues that may need attention, sing through tricky rhythms, preferably using Solfa.
- Analyse what structures and patterns are in the music, for example, scales, arpeggios, chromatics, repetitions, dominant 7th chords—all of which are in the line below.

- Sing or say aloud and finger the notes. Play the notes in equal time—without rhythm. Then play the rhythm on bongo drums. Join rhythm and notes together.
- Play out–of–time. Don't move from one note or chord until absolutely sure of the next.
- The Add–a–Bit Method: Isolate the tricky passage. Start with a manageable few notes. Add a block of notes, and then progress with further segments.
- De–scribble: As a student and fledgling teacher I drew lavish scribbles to alert mistakes. It was confronting to play offending passages and I felt my brain go into spasm to decipher right from wrong. Now in my teaching and playing I am thrifty with pencil markings. A small dash indicates a change of direction in a pattern of notes or sequences; a yellow pencil (*not* permanent highlighter) draws the eye to an error. Too much information can be counterproductive.
- Simplify: Adhesive whiteouts are useful to boost my basic accompanying skills; thick chords can be reduced to 2–noters.
- The 10–in–a–Row *Snakes and Ladders* Game: Play the tricky passage correctly 10 consecutive times to be foolproof. If you slip on the ninth time, it's down the snake to start all over again.
- Pianists should play each hand separately. Try to play one hand and sing the other part.
- Photocopy difficult passages, enlarged to A3 size: Tape your student's performance of this. Listen back and highlight any mistakes with a fluorescent pen. Analyse the weak spots, why they lost the plot. Divide crucial connections into bite–size bits and they repeat these over and over. A week later repeat the process and admire the improvement between the two pages. Give them a jellybean.

Making music–reading as easy as ABC

Phil Davis, Head of Music at Redlands College, Queensland, writes:

For fluent note reading, students need to learn how to predict and interpret the symbols of written music and to scan ahead with frequent glances. This establishes expectation of what the written music could be as the written 'clues' unfold.

Poor music reading skills in students usually stem scenarios such as: The student who will stop when he/she plays or sings a wrong note, or is uncertain what note to play or sing. Here the student stops to correct the pitch (spelling) of an isolated note (word) when an error occurs, rather than reading through the musical phrase (sentence) and finding its musical meaning overall (context).

- ***Plan your journey before playing****: Check the oil, water and tyres. Note and prepare for the requirements of key and time signatures, speed, mood, accidentals, dynamics, technical and any rhythmical demands.*
- ***Play****: Keep driving at a steady speed. There is a 'rightness' in music reading that can be acquired— no different to learning to read a book without having to stop every time you find a word that cannot be spelt or understood fully.*
- ***Refine and Revise****: Slow down while you improve your driving skills. Correct and refine pitch or particular rhythms as a micro study in the learning process. In this stage, attention is given to smaller detail, for example pencilled reminders of fingerings, or where the beats fall in a particular bar. Isolate technical difficulties and play slowly. This highlights the learning outcomes for students as they process the detail through selective study and revision of those playing areas needing specific corrections.*

As the students unify the above aspects they become competent and fluent. They gain confidence and home practice becomes more worthwhile, achievable and sustainable.

I recommend starting the above strategies with material of one or two lines' duration only using simple rhythms, limited dynamic changes and easy melodic material. Singing or playing along helps, but the main purpose is to teach the musician to process information by reading ahead and to keep going to the end of the sight reading exercise irrespective of errors on the way. Repeat the process one or two times more and reinforce improvements as they are made, and set specific goals by isolating any areas as needed.

Rebuilding musical memory

Tom Beek suggests that if there's a certain passage that students play 'wrong' all the time, the passage gets stuck in their memory as 'here I always screw up.' He suggests 'To avoid that pattern, I give high priority to re–condition their musical memory. But of course they can only do this themselves. They have to feel they can do it, and build confidence out of that. A good way is to resize the hard chunk into small parts.

'Singing works well. It filters out the first distractions and other misbalance from playing the instrument. So when they're ready to play (and read), their mind is clean'.

Chapter 20
Make technique palatable

No pupil can really progress unless a secure foundation is built with a necessary balance of 'technique' and musical enjoyment. Choose varied, melodic studies. Give reasons why they will improve playing. Set goals to reach.

Where possible, I like to camouflage exercises as melodic, fun pieces; my students love the Mystery Melody concept in *Enjoy Playing the Clarinet* which teases them to extend their fingerwork. For beginners it gives a good opportunity to sound flashy with notes that lie under the fingers.

What is more important: to create in our pupils good exercise or good piece players? Yet surely they must master technical problems through etudes and exercises rather than lovely repertoire. How to present these in an enticing manner?

A television commercial gave good advice: 'Don't tell them it's healthy and they'll eat it by the bagful.' Persuade your students that music–making is recreation, enjoyment and fulfilling. If they are rewarded for an intensive improvement campaign with beautiful pieces they will surge forward through the valleys.

Beethoven summed up the ideals of good teaching from a viewpoint of guardian, musician, composer and teacher. He wrote to Czerny about his nephew Carl's piano lessons, asking him for patience and to be kind, yet serious—or Carl would accomplish less:

...If once he has got the right fingering, plays in good time, with the notes fairly correct, then only pull him up about the rendering; and when he has arrived at that stage, don't let him stop for the sake of small faults, but point them out to him when he has played the piece through... I have always adopted this plan; it soon forms musicians which, after all, is one of the first aims. of art and it gives less trouble both to master and pupil. (Hamburger: p.153-4)

Demystify scales—and make them happen

Is there anything more indigestible in music (even, in life) than playing scales? Yet we teachers insist our students work at them every day.

Are scales dead? Education syllabi tend to dumb down the more unpleasant but necessary foundations. Thus students lack a solid technical basis. Have teachers and publishers succumbed to screen–addicted Generation Y's reluctance to face the 'boring stuff'? We should not assume so. Some quite enjoy the routine of playing scales but, if we don't nominate them, why should they be included in a practice regime?

Such questions came to the fore when I reviewed Book 2 of an instrumental method whose only whiff of a scale was one octave of C major. Was I optimistic, naïve, even draconian to take beginners through to E major in my method *Enjoy Playing the Clarinet*? (It was crafty to include E major '*In the Mood*' to work out arpeggios over register crossings.)

The reviewed method challenges players with attractive, tricky pieces in keys of three or four sharps but without the technical preparation of relevant scales. It includes interesting rhythms, encourages listening, ensemble and performance. And practice. But what *do* they practise? Apparently not scales, arpeggios or even exercises that would increase fluency. My students learn new pieces only after first playing their relevant scales.

Do teachers choose a method book according to the enjoyment level? Or do they value books that include technical pages that can be skipped by less motivated players? Let's mount a campaign to retain technical expectations.

One way to build technique is to enlist students for examinations, which will require performance of scales and arpeggios. Tell them from me that examiners are most impressed by candidates who play accurate technical work the *first* time. Don't rely on restarts which only cause them to fluster and also run the examiner late.

Students must understand and remember key signatures, patterns and structures. With a new key, I have my pupils say or sing aloud while they finger, one octave at a time, before they play.

This is because scales make little sense on a clarinet, unlike the piano, where players can see the notes and the scale patterns in front of them. A keyboard player routinely produces new intervals of varied width by moving just one finger. The clarinettist may move three fingers, or even all 10, but with illogical results; move one thumb and leap an interval of 12 notes, yet a half–tone's difference can be produced by moving three fingers.

At least woodwind players lift or drop their fingers according to whether the pitch ascends or descends. Mostly. Pity the trumpeters—there is no such logic in their finger movements. String players follow patterns, and rely on their ear. Players of all other instruments except keyboard have few visible structures to guide them. They have to think what comes next, note–by–note, and draw on knowledge of key signatures.

Scale practice is best at slow speed so accurate notes are imprinted into the memory bank. Then, if some nerves intrude in performance, they can go onto autopilot and reproduce the correct notes.

Use the analogy that competitors warm up before sports events, so their muscles are primed for action. So too, should musicians.

There are extensive tips in my book *Practice is a Dirty Word; How to clean up your act* and in my eBook *Music Scales: Tips to make them happen*.

Chapter 21
Preparing students for examinations

At the beginning of a year or semester, or with new students, discuss with them whether an examination is an option and when it might be feasible. Demonstrate possible pieces so the pupil can choose which ones appeal. My students will learn twice as many pieces as are required, so a month before the big date we can decide which are most fluent, polished and which display the student's strengths. This avoids staleness and maintains momentum. Various new challenges can be explored and conquered.

Exams are a good goal as they ensure regular practice of scales and arpeggios. We hope. Before a holiday, we set the student a plan for each week's actions and achievements. Will we be disappointed at the next lesson? Some still produce warm resonant tone and mobile fingers. Others left their scales in the too–hard basket.

'What's melodic again?' asks one. Grit teeth.

'All year I've written up notes of harmonic and melodic scales in your notebook.'

'Lost it.'

'Where are your post–it notes, I gave you two sandwich bags; one labelled 'work in progress,' the other 'in the bag.' Remember?'

Doesn't want to know. Sigh. Pull out more felt pens and post–it notes.

'If you really work, you could nail these in time,' I rally.

A chasm lies between 'could' and 'will.' We can rave and rant, bounce off ceilings, but unless the student follows up at home there is no progress. They must take ownership of their own practice.

A *eureka* moment hits me. Did the student write the scale names on the post–it notes or did I? Is my mistake that I'm the active partner; as long as I turn conniptions and somersaults to make it happen, the student can stay passive?

'Don't do for students what they can do for themselves,' I remind myself. Why do I pencil numbers or strokes for beats above the notes? Let them write it and I will discover just how hazy is their understanding. I know rhythm; they don't. They will not master it as long as I think for them. We clap rhythms together. They should clap alone first, then I will join them to clarify.

Post–it power

I am the queen of post–it notes. They have many uses:

A passage that bristles with accidentals is easier to face if two post–it notes form a window. This can be moved to extend the view as notes are added. This is helpful for students of clarinet who are daunted by enharmonics. They can learn a few notes at a time.

I eschew scale books as being no–brainers. Instead I write (or the student does) the names of scales, each on post–it notes. Each key's major, harmonic and melodic scales, arpeggios and related chords are colour coded. I write accidentals in red so they can't be ignored.

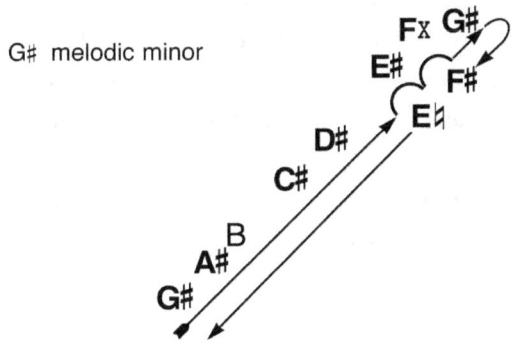

Perform accurate scales

I hold regular 'Scaleathons' well before examinations so young students consistently learn technical work and can perform it correctly with ready response.

- Agree on a list of scales to be prepared, write their names on pieces of paper to be drawn from a hat.
- Each player starts with a kitty of jellybeans. In turn, each contestant plays the scale selected from the hat: if correct the first time, they win a jellybean; if incorrect a jellybean is forfeited. ('No, Amanda, you can't have half a jellybean because it was half–correct! It's either right or wrong. Alex, you only get a jelly bean if it's correct the first time.')
- Wind up with improvisation, sight–reading or a jam session.

This mix of fun and friendly rivalry fans an incentive to practice far better than any nagging I might do. Students learn to produce scales correctly the first time, under light–hearted performance pressure. The bottom line is that they can perform them accurately and on demand while still having some fun.

My students know that there will be high expectations from me in the weeks prior to a performance. However, by the final lesson the spadework should be done. This is not the time for a bewildering barrage of: 'What's the key signature of g# minor? Remember the alternate fingerings; count carefully and don't rush!' I like to lighten the tension by sending them off with relaxed parting words like: 'Whatever happens, play beautifully and enjoy yourself.' Or, for clarinet players: 'If you squeak, make it a good one!'

It avails little to flood the student with a wash of reminders and negative criticisms at this stage. It may paralyse them and cripple the positive work of months. Send them off with positive words and encouragement singing in their ears.

There is more information about preparation and performance in my book *Confident Music Performance*.

Chapter 22
Offer performance opportunities

Accustom students to the challenges of performance with a studio concert in a comfortable environment, before progressing to more demanding situations. Several weeks before the exam or competition, it's a good idea for the students to run through the whole program in front of a relaxed audience of their family, other students, the cat, and enlisted neighbours. They can wind up with some fun ensemble work. Regular sight–reading ensemble sessions allow the students to enjoy playing together while developing ensemble skills.

The student is announced in an official voice. A bow is given. Stage presentation is practised until it comes naturally. I write comments, as an examiner would do. They develop the stamina required to play whole pieces through, and then have time to improve any weak areas. I present each student with a small memento, treat or certificate.

A painful memory of a mishap in public can entrench resistance to future performances. The best place to overcome this is a friendly studio concert. Reassure them that even Beethoven experienced a bad experience. Louis Spohr described Beethoven's disaster performance of his Pianoforte Concerto. At the first *sforzando* he threw out his arms so wide that he knocked both the lights off the piano upon the ground. When the audience laughed, Beethoven was so incensed at this disturbance that he made the orchestra stop and begin again. The mishaps continued, though: two boys stood either side of

Beethoven to hold the lights. At the fatal *sforzando* one of the boys *'received from Beethoven's out–thrown right hand so smart a blow on the mouth, that he dropped the light in terror.'* (Spohr: 1969). The audience's 'bacchanalian roar' of laughter so angered Beethoven that at the first chords of his solo, half a dozen strings broke. This embarrassing performance experience drove Beethoven from the concert platform forever. What a waste.

Take heart. If a towering genius such as Beethoven was mortified on–stage, we should feel heartened that our less dramatic mishaps will fade to insignificance. Use all your tact to enquire if a painful memory holds your student back as a musician. If so:

- Was the incident an accident (as was Beethoven's)?
- Was it preventable?
- If *yes* to the latter:
- Why did it occur? Lack of practice, of rehearsal, focus or technique?
- What technical foundation will you put in place before a repeat performance?
- What steps could you take to surmount this bad experience?
- How have you improved and matured since then?
- Here are some suggestions to help pupils resolve that murky memory:
- Relearn that piece, at half–speed and relaxed. You may find it easier than you remember as your technique and experience have since grown.
- Record it and listen back to your playing. Not so bad, hmm? Which bars need 80% of your time?
- Play an informal, no–sweat performance of the piece to a few friends and family.
- Celebrate afterwards, for you are a survivor. Feel proud that you have overcome a bad experience. You have one up on poor Beethoven!

The teacher's approach can make all the difference after a student experiences a poor performance. We can talk them through afterwards to build confidence for the next one. They may expect a barrage of recriminations. Surprise them by instead asking, 'What went well in your performance? What was better than you expected?' After they have found some positives: 'And what will you do better next time?'

A high-achieving student, Nicole, was upset because she didn't bring the piano accompaniment to an eisteddfod; her previous accompanist had always brought it. She played unaccompanied, but with less brilliance than usual. When I asked her what she did well, she shook her head. Nothing. 'But you didn't run out the back door, you went onstage and did your best, right?' A small nod. 'That shows you are a trooper, a professional. This was not your fault; in fact it was no one's. But what did you learn from the experience?' She will bring the piano book next time.

'What was your percentage of accuracy?' High, now she thought about it. Nicole left the room with a lighter step and looks forward to the next competition.

Brain Gym and Applied Kinesiology

Performers strive to play their best, but excess zeal is self–defeating. The essence of trying involves doubt. The analytical left–brain is not only a critic, but also a doubter. I tell my students to 'switch off your try–hard button.' Focus awareness on one single aspect of the playing. As passive observation is a right brain activity, it allows one to escape the critical and doubting words of the left–brain. Exchange mental self–talk to 'try' or 'make an effort' for positives like 'experiment' or 'challenge.'

These concepts are central to Educational Kinesiology, pioneered by educator and author Paul E. Dennison and his wife Gail. Their program, *Brain Gym*, was conceived to correct learning disabilities. In it, simple movements and Laterality Repatterning enable people to access those parts of the brain that were inaccessible to them. Walking is a form of 'cross–crawl.' The action of crossing the centre–line enables whole–brain learning and expression. In the 'old days' when students marched into class, their brains were primed and ready to receive information.

When students struggle to solve a problem, getting worse instead of better, here's a tip to break the downward cycle; make a pretext to turn aside, to rummage in the music cupboard. Or boil the kettle for a cup of tea, while they play the passage by themselves. It will improve. Lighten the focus on their weakness, and they feel free to process the information. Choose your battles and don't overload.

Encourage for optimum results:

The word encourage means to 'give them courage'. Even when a student has made a very poor showing in a lesson, when tough words have been necessary, it is important to balance the criticism with positive reinforcement.

Honey, rather than vinegar, attracts the bees. Find—even invent, if really pushed—some small aspect to praise in the student's work and watch the change in their body language, confidence and interest. You will achieve far more dramatic results than a half–hour's nagging over numerous details. Try it: 'What an expressive phrase you played! I loved the echoes.' Maybe the student did not mean to play an echo, but the whole piece will now resound with them.

Avoid the words 'good' and 'bad' because neither tell you what to continue working with and what to try to fix. Identify both what behaviour we want to replace and then what we want to happen instead. Focus is then on what we *want* to happen, rather than what went wrong. Highlight what went right and how to repeat it.

'When I say x, what does that mean to you?' Before I write in the student's journal, I check how they would like me to write down something in their journal.

Encourage them with 'I like that, can I hear it again?'

Yes, I know. We all encounter some horror students who try our patience to the limit, whose granite faces and sounds quell our most stimulating, creative, positive ideas. Our best efforts to discover and address the reasons seem useless. If students do become discouraged, reassure them—and ourselves!—that such phases are inevitable sometimes.

Even Beethoven wept over his early lessons, and both Weber and Wagner were told that they would never amount to anything in music. Brilliant prodigy as he was, Mozart wrote, 'As soon as people lose confidence in me, I am apt to lose confidence in myself.' (Mozart Letters, p.79)

Some of my best teacher training has come from my sons. Motherhood has made me a more tolerant, understanding teacher. Of course both roles have cost sleep at times.

Focus on the positives during torrid times. List '*Things I like about you*' or write up the '*good news*' after a child's Parent–Teacher meetings in which all agreed: 'He could be an A student if only he worked harder.'

Express negatives in a manner that still allows people to feel good about themselves. Create situations where students feel good about themselves. Even when a pupil has made a poor showing in a lesson, when tough words have been necessary, it's important to balance criticism with encouragement. It's less wear–and–tear on teachers as well as the students. Find a seed of good in each student. Nurture this fragile plant so it thrives. We can enjoy watching the growth.

The perfection trap

The biggest single cause of nerves, insecurity, low self–esteem and depression is the perfection goal. It can cause even the most capable, prepared and talented presenters to give up.

I am allergic to the admonishment 'Practice makes perfect.' Relax students with the words 'Please don't try to be perfect. None of us can be a hundred percent perfect, not even top mega–performers.' None of us can be perfect this side of the grave.

- Show them another angle: *Intelligent thoughtful practice may make near perfect.*
- Instead of striving for perfection, give them a new do–able goal:
- 'Aim for excellence. Create habits of excellence.'

Such attitudes free their creativity to flow.

We are what we repeatedly do. Excellence then, is not an act, but a habit.
– Aristotle.

Chapter 23
Prime students to work with accompanists

Those teachers who are fluent pianists have an advantage in that they can accompany instrumentalists during lessons so they gain the full musical experience. Some can pick out a few chords in lessons but have the sense to enlist a professional for performances.

Prime students before a rehearsal with an accompanist. Younger ones are unused to asserting themselves with those they see as more senior, experienced and respected. They need to be encouraged to see that this is their performance and they should not endure an unaccustomed tempo because the pianist set this. Accompanists are long–suffering stalwarts who without a blink follow soloists through rough *rubati* and wonky rhythms. Value a good pianist. Never take them for granted or 'ride them'. The following points will enhance productive and successful interaction with our pianists.

- Study the piano part; play some bars if possible.
- Pencil rhythmic cues into your part to assist entries.
- Give clear up–beats—in the tempo they really mean.
- Eye contact and body language builds trust and helps with vagrant beats.
- Trust the pianist to follow through mishaps.
- Before you start to play, mentally sing the opening phrase so that you

establish the speed at which you are comfortable. Or if the score starts with a piano introduction, first play a few bars to demonstrate your tempo.
- Point out that experienced pianists are quick to catch your tempo as long as you give clear signals, with uncluttered body language. Beware of giving mixed signals, like a toe that taps an unconscious cross–rhythm. Most accompanists can pick up a tempo from the speed of wind players' and singers' breath intakes, so be sure to breathe in the tempo. String players give body upbeats.
- Meaningful eye contact adds security as well as clear ensemble. Angle yourself so you can see each other.

Time counts

Allow plenty of rehearsal time rather than rely on pianists' listening skills—or even powers of extrasensory perception. It is obvious to an examiner when student and pianist have met for the first time in the warm–up room. However, in the real world, there are times when experienced musicians have to cope with 'one run through and on with the show'.

Rehearsals are most fruitful if you know the music inside out—both your own part and, just as important, the piano's interaction. Listen to recordings and live performances of the work. Practise from the score so you can see what is going on. Pencil in crucial rhythmic cues so that you know what to listen for at entries. Be specific in asking for help with eye–contact cues.

What if the pianist sets the wrong tempo in an introduction?

Your students need to be forewarned how to rescue such a situation: Weber's Concertino for clarinet begins with an introduction. Imagine if the orchestral conductor or pianist, as the case may be, has set a tempo too fast or too slow. As you enter with a sustained note, there is little opportunity to adjust the tempo. Frantic gestures and time beating would destroy the nuanced mood of that first phrase, your own poise and the audience's enjoyment. Eye contact may work the trick, otherwise allow the pianist to continue playing the intro, then after the long note, assert the exact tempo you want, backed with eye contact and decisive body language. Expect the accompanist to follow you. Such confidence rescues a misjudged tempo.

What if I come unstuck from my pianist mid–piece?

Even a prepared and experienced player can upset ensemble by slips, jump a line, or forget that *Da Capo*. Mixed signals, such as a toe–tapping at a different tempo, may lose the plot.

If you make a mistake, resist the temptation to go back and pick up that lost note or beat, or you may both search for each other in the frightening fog of no–man's land. Keep going with steady rhythm and rely on the pianist to find you. Good pianists can jump a beat, bar or line without the slightest flicker to give the game away. They see the big picture with the solo line in their score. They accept that it is their role to reconnoitre, yours to lead.

A time to listen—and a time to just count

Teachers stress that students must listen, not rely on the pianist to follow. Soloists must know when the accompaniment changes pulse, for example from duple to triple time. With cross–rhythms and hectic fast movements, listening may be counter–productive; keep your nerve, a steady beat and forge ahead.

Don't shoot the pianist!

Good accompanists are pure gold! Nurture your relationships, and they'll be there for you. They will follow you through obscure modulations and Dal Segno signs. Treasure the one who breathes and thinks with you, who will jump bars to follow any memory lapses or confusions.

Keep your pianist on side and save rehearsal time–wastage by being efficient and well–prepared. A student may become blacklisted in the accompanying fraternity if they:

- Walk into the first and only rehearsal bearing a virtuosic piece with the nonchalant words: 'What am I playing? Oh, did you want to see it first?' (Give or send the music to your accompanist at least two weeks before the performance. Pianists must cover much fierce repertoire in busy times like examination or audition seasons. Nasty little surprises can upset the equilibrium of even the most fluent and virtuosic fingers.)
- Each rehearsal, change your mind back and forth about the best breathing points. Borrow their pencil and eraser to change on your part. (Mark your breathing points in the piano score. Warn them of bars

where performance pressures may require an extra breath or leeway.)
- Change tempi according to whim or the difficulty of the notes. (Mark any tempo and dynamic changes or extra ones.)
- Send a text message just before the performance to notify that the venue is at the other side of town from what you'd indicated. (Note the time, date and place of the performance on a post–it slip of paper, or perhaps on the music.)
- After playing a difficult duo, bow and milk applause, but keep the pianist skulking on the piano bench. (Acknowledge your accompanist at the end of the performance. The piano part is often as demanding as the solo part, if not more so.)
- Say after the recital: 'Oh, did you expect to be paid?' (Ask what the fee will be and have it ready after the performance.)

Treat your accompanists with respect as professionals and they will play with you again. Working as a team, your relationships develop as you breathe, feel and flow together. Then you will better enjoy the depths and riches of playing ensemble music. Playing a single line instrument without full harmony is bare and thin. Enjoy the camaraderie and music!

Gerald Moore, arguably one of the most esteemed accompanists in living memory, felt decimated by his early experiences. A singer reduced him to such a state of nerves that he could hardly play a simple introduction without errors. What if such an agonising experiences had caused this—eventually—respected pianist to conclude he had 'something wrong with him' and to give up? What a loss it would have been! (Moore: 1962)

Think... Do you have dreamy students who appear 'away with the fairies', behind the beat, non–compos mentis? Maybe they have abilities not yet revealed to you.

Chapter 24
Help for nervous students

Let us not destroy the love of performing in our zeal to be a 'good' teacher. Let's take care as we submit our students for yet more competitions. Does our ego hunger for recognition? Do students welcome each opportunity, or might over–exposure develop an allergy to performance? They will best develop their own potential if they *enjoy* their music.

How can we help when students express qualms? We help them face examinations, competitions, and concerts when we pass on our own experiences of conquering performance problems.

Consider whether we extend them too far or too fast. Elsewhere I recommend a challenge to spark interest. However, we need to know the abilities and responses of students before we do so. It is a tricky balance and, on the other hand, we must not pressure them beyond their capability.

I see this especially when students skip examination grades. If they receive an A for grade four with glowing comments from the examiner, it is misguided to send them back later in the year to sit grade seven. Greater finesse, technical prowess and maturity will be expected at higher grades. It is a pity to skip pleasant repertoire of the other grades that would also build technique and stamina.

We help them to develop discipline necessary to realise their potential. It seems rough justice that many of the most gifted are the least disciplined. As a result, teachers may see exceptional talents slip like eels out of their fingers. Meanwhile, those of lesser ability may achieve high standards by sheer tenacity. Later we will look at ways to motivate.

Prepare for peak performance

Remember the kindergarten song 'Head, shoulders, knees and toes'? Use this easy framework to remember simple holistic tips to power up public performances:

1. **Head**: Successful performance starts at the top. Firstly, be tough with your head. Edit out any self–sabotaging head talk. Strength lies in appreciating our strengths rather than focusing on mistakes. See elsewhere about Emotional Freedom Technique.
Tell students to calm with a hand on the forehead and slow breaths. This action clears 'brain–fog' memory lapses, increases clarity and focus, while diffusing excess adrenaline jitters. It releases stress and brings energy away from the fight/flight brainstem, and towards the neo–cortex, where rational thought occurs.
2. **Shoulders**: Under pressure we protectively hunch our shoulders. Or they lift, a sure sign of shallow breathing. Drop the shoulders and give them turtle shrugs to relax.
3. **Knees**: Many standing performers lock their knees, which transmits excess tension through the whole body. Slightly bend and soften the knees; this eases any tense stomach and throat muscles and improves vocal tone.
4. **Toes**: If standing, balance square on two feet for a secure foundation.

Your brain, breath and body are tuned for a positive poised and confident performance.

Face the Shakes

Many students when asked, 'What is your deepest, murkiest fear as this performance looms?' nominate the shakes. String players dread wobbly bow strokes, vocalists that unintended vibrato. Shaky fingers or lips inhibit many instrumentalists. Such jitters seem painfully obvious to the performers and it is small comfort that many listeners are oblivious.

Our society tends to silence problems with pills rather than find a solution.

'Beta–blocker' drugs block the adrenaline reaction and anxiety symptoms by slowing the heart rate to reduce sweating and tremors. They do not stop nerves, but lessen the symptoms by slowing the heart rate. Medical prescription is essential as they can be dangerous for people prone to diabetes, certain heart conditions, bronchitis, depression, hay fever and asthma. Test suitability well before a performance; it would be shattering to discover an unsuspected cardiac or asthma condition onstage. Reported side effects include dizziness, light–headedness, nightmares, hallucinations, lethargy, insomnia, visual disturbances, diarrhoea, drowsiness, cold hands and feet.

Instead, offer students these practical solutions:

- **Give yourself permission to shake**: The more we try to control shaking, the worse it gets. Instead, take the paradoxical approach. Rather than fight against shakes, allow yourself to do so: 'You want to shake, fingers. Well, go on—shake.' Some performers consciously make their hands tremble or their knees shake as a way of trying to produce the symptom rather than conceal it. Jittery fingers may result from excess adrenal energy. Backstage, give your hands a brisk rub and shake them.
- **Diversionary Tactics**: Direct your thoughts onto another aspect of your performance. Our mind resists thinking of two things at once. Focus on your strengths, not weaknesses.
- **Change of focus**: Transfer your nervous energy away from the tense part of your body (for example, your jaw). Think 'toes, toes' and your jaw relaxes. This was proved true by American summer music camp organist and clarinettist, John Allegar. In our coaching session he admitted to suffering every nervous symptom possible. After his subsequent performance I congratulated him on his poise and calm, he said, 'My hands shook in the beginning, then I remembered you said to focus on my toes and that helped, till they shook a little. So I focused back onto my hands and soon the piece finished.' He won his competition with high commendation and is now a doctoral candidate at Eastman School of Music. His update is: 'They haven't altogether left me, but they are in check. A complete lack of them, I think, takes away some of our fire. It's a life's work to turn them into positive performance energy.'

Chapter 25
Help Students to shine in performance

A holistic Brain – Breath – Body pre–performance preparation offers positive, natural ways to combat nerves.

BRAIN

Success or failure is determined at the top, in our heads, to visualise success and channel adrenaline into energy.

Tell your students:
- In the days, hours, minutes before your performance, visualise yourself succeeding: 'I feel fine, my fingers and shoulders are relaxed. I've prepared and am in good form.'
- Edit out those belittling voices in your head. (It's not schizophrenia, but those finger–pointing, accusing negatives we all experience at times.)
- Picture your playing as effortless, musical, brilliant.
- See yourself winning—and you may create a self–fulfilling prophecy.

Diffuse excess adrenaline with Brain Gym's 'Positive Points' technique (http://www.braingym.org) Place a hand on your forehead, inhaling deeply. This simple action encourages blood flow to the frontal lobes where rational thought occurs. It curbs fight or flight jitters, releases memory blocks and enables you to walk onto the platform accessing your whole brain. If memory slips intrude mid–performance, simply pause between movements, breathe deeply with a hand to your forehead and regain focus. Hold these emotional stress–release neurovascular balance points of the stomach meridian. This also curbs stomach queasiness.

BREATH

The very word 'inspiration' relates to breath. Slow deep breaths help us calm, poise and focus. Backstage before the performance, exhale a big gusty sigh until your lungs feel quite empty. Inhale. Repeat several times.

Relax and encourage deep, easy and natural breathing with the Alexander Technique's 'whispered ahh.' Stand balanced and upright. Smile broadly showing the teeth, which touch but are unclenched. Let your jaw swing open as you exhale on a whispered 'ahh'—the purest, uninterrupted sound you can make. This energising oxygen intake relaxes your jaw, improves projection and tone, eases tension and nausea. This is a subtle preparation during those minutes backstage. The benefits are that it:

- Allows more oxygen into the blood stream.
- Helps release stale air at bottom of lungs.
- Prevents tension caused by shallow breathing.
- Eases nausea, seasickness, even hangover.
- Eases dry mouth as it increases saliva flow.

During your performance, remember to breathe often; at cadences, between movements, as phrases rise to their climax. String players can inhale on up–bows and exhale on down–bows. Singers, wind and brass players do not have a premium of air. When keyboard and string players are reminded to breathe, their music gains surprising flow and resonance.

BODY

When confronted by a performance situation, a common instinct is to hunch and huddle, which shortens the spine. Command the room with upright posture by standing against a wall before walking onstage. Stretch and yawn. Walk on as a winner.

Professional poise is essential for competitions. Audiences and juries assess your manner, posture, eye contact and body language as well as your musical notes. When I adjudicate competitions, I can predict a good or a poor performance before a single note has been played. Body language reveals confidence—or lack of it. Performers who slink on–stage, wishing they were elsewhere, should expand their chests and smile. Listeners will believe us if our body language says, 'Listen to me: I am the greatest!' We may even fool ourselves!

Seven easy habits for confident performance

These doable tips can help students to channel adrenalin away from survival fight or flight mode into focus and electricity so they shine in performance. Remind them to enjoy their music. Perhaps defuse with laughter but use caution, as it can be misinterpreted or counterproductive for those in a sensitised state. Encouraging right–brain listening skills and expressive communication helps them to *express* the imprinting (*impress*) of past lessons and practice.

Students who access their cerebral cortex rather than the primitive brain–stem mode are better able to perform to the best of their ability. Encourage right–brain listening skills and expressive communication. Help them to express the imprinting (impress) of past lessons and practice with these habits, more fully explained elsewhere:

1. Prepare (Fail to Prepare = Prepare to Fail).
2. Positive thoughts: We are what we think so banish defeatist thoughts. Emotional Freedom Technique curbs self–sabotage.
3. 'Positive points: A hand on your forehead, with deep breathing, calms tremors, channels into frontal lobes of clear thought, clears 'brain fog.'
4. Yawn (backstage), stretch and breathe.
5. Walk (which is cross–crawl) for circulation, and to activate whole–brain response.
6. Water intake helps us to think clearly. Singers and speakers benefit as it lubricates vocal folds.
7. Positive posture projects confidence. Stand tall against a backstage wall.

They can walk onto the platform feeling relatively positive and draw on their practice and preparation to produce a star performance.

During the performance

What do we remember most about a performance? The mistakes. It is a pity that such emphasis is placed on a negative, rather than remember the positives of beautiful tone and flowing expression. Here are some ways to play to our optimum ability and preparation:
- If standing, soften your knees, balance square on both feet. Or sit upright.
- Be kind to yourself. An occasional error, stumble or mistake does not spell doom to the performance.
- Forgive the odd wobbly note, squeak, mistake—people may focus on your rich tone and musicianship and miss the errors.
- Play out with big full tone.
- Exaggerate dynamics.
- Breathe!
- Aim for excellence—not perfection.
- Communicate with your listeners.
- Enjoy your music!

Chapter 26
Help your students handle critiques and criticism

Teachers can prepare pupils for inevitable negatives they will encounter as they develop. Performing artists must learn to cope with criticism or find a less challenging day job.

How can we cope when comments hurt and inhibit us even to the extent of destroying our self–confidence? It depends on how the words were directed. Criticism may come from within us or without and can be positive or negative, constructive or destructive.

Sources of criticism and strategies for coping

Probably the most unkind voices we ever encounter come from inside our own minds. Don't many of us sometimes feel beaten by that running commentary on our performance which notices the negative aspects far more often than the positive?

We all have some such voices flitting through our conscious mind, but we do not need to allow them to belittle us. Monitor them closely and shut off any phrases which begin with 'I should,' 'I never' and 'I ought'. Addressing yourself as 'you' or 's/he'sounds less hard than 'I' statements. When your thoughts criticise harshly, block them with a simple directive 'Stop!' See yourself sitting at the console of your mind. You can choose to turn up the volume of the positive thoughts, to turn down the negative ones or, better still, switch off the tape.

Or shift the focus to another aspect of your playing, away from the 'stressor'. For example, if your thoughts run along these lines, 'All those people in the audience must think I'm dreadful to make so many mistakes!', tell yourself that it is good they are there to pay your fee. If the stressor is fear of a difficult passage, move to a less stressful thought: 'What does the author/composer want me to express here?' or 'What a lovely harmony he created here.'

As well as learning to cope with these internal voices, we need to learn to deal with external ones.

Our performance has gone well so far. Smiles from the audience and clapping. Except at interval. As we are stoking up our courage for the next tricky piece, a colleague comes up and in a devastatingly helpful guise says, 'Pity about the intonation' (as happened once to the cellist in our quartet), or 'Had a bit of a problem with the balance, did you?'

Up until now we've been perfectly happy with the intonation and balance and so is the critic, as we discover in the paper – if we are fortunate to receive a critique. We don't know that now and we have to walk on stage for the second half of that tricky solo. We feel shattered, angry. Of course, we do. Let's not be unrealistic.

We don't have much time to indulge in this, however. We have to rally with some response. Try a bland 'thank you for your feedback,' and beat a fast retreat to save giving some satisfaction. Or perhaps, if feeling relatively confident and strong add, 'But in what way? How do you suggest I improve?' And see how shallow this judgment was.

We need to stoke ourselves with positive thoughts. Tell yourself that no-one kicks a dead dog. There has to be some reason, hopefully positive, which needled such an attack. Try to feel sorry for the person. After all, how much has that person proved in a career? No doubt some inadequaces are the cause of this.

In the case which we experienced, it was fortunate that a much more respected colleague and teacher came backstage soon after and complimented our cellist, not only for her wonderful playing, but on her stunning appearance.

She did not share this criticism with us until after the concert, which was wise as it would have unsettled the whole group.

It helps to have thought through such issues so they don't catch us totally open–mouthed. Unfortunately, we will encounter colleagues who are quite prepared to use whatever means to bring us down. I have noticed that top artists often appear genuinely open, generous, less prone to backbiting. (Perhaps because a tame dragon mother–in–law or wife guards their time and their access by telephone. Useful trick, that.)

In competitive careers, there are always people who are quick to judge and loudly. Those in orchestras, theatre companies, opera choruses, corps de ballets are thrown into constant, quite intimate relationships of interdependence with colleagues. How can we escape from the influence of that cocksure, abrasive, self–centred person who shares a dressing room or sits in the next chair? Touring means constant contact, during which a simple personality clash can be aggravated to intolerable proportions.

The Desiderata advises us to 'avoid loud and aggressive persons, for they are a vexation to the spirit.' But short of changing jobs, we cannot do so, for they are always in close physical proximity. We need to develop other strategies.

Some people are like parasites whose greatest talent appears to be the ability to feed on our energy, to drain us and sap our confidence. They have an instinct for our weak spots and bring us down with a few well–chosen words.

Our natural instinct is to deny them, to refuse to listen, or to throw up a smokescreen of lavish explanations. We may be stung into striking back with equally cruel barbs, getting embroiled in an argument, spitting words which lose respect on both sides. Such tactics complicate and damage the relationships more.

It is difficult to do so, but we must mentally create invisible boundaries or 'space bubbles' around ourselves beyond which they cannot reach us. Imagine a perspex or glass partition in the space between the chairs. Imagine cotton wool (or steel wool!) in our ears, which deflects the criticisms back onto them. Or see their little barbs bouncing off our head without leaving so much as a dint. Perhaps you could grow an imaginary outer skin layer like a bandaid?

Don't we all recognise this situation? With faultless timing, just when we are feeling most insecure, that loud–mouth neatly lobs a barbed criticism into our most vulnerable tender spot. Or two harsh words in a review destroy our fragile self–esteem.

Of course these words hurt. It would be silly to pretend otherwise. Or would it?

Develop some tactics and especially a talent for acting:

Act deaf. You didn't hear them. Pretend to ignore them. A good trick when someone is verbally attacking you is to break eye contact by looking to one side or out the window.

Act bored. So what? Who's listening to you?

Defuse their ammunition by agreeing with them some aspect while not putting yourself down. 'Yes, I have played better. But didn't you notice I handled the last few minutes really well?' Stun them by acting out of the usual. By acknowledging one part of their comments, you throw them off–guard. The question challenges them, perhaps puts them on the wrong foot by implying that their own listening was remiss. From a position of strength, move in to affirm your own positives.

Resist the urge to put them down in turn. Say, 'I respect your opinion, but…'

Or throw the onus back onto them with: 'How do you suggest I improve it?' Keep all traces of criticism out of your voice. You may be surprised by the answer. Perhaps they have a useful, positive comment to make and we have misread their attitude.

An effective antidote for criticism is generosity. If we do not sink to their level, if we are fair and generous with our praise, people are less likely to feel defensive in our company. Remember, what we give out comes back to us.

If someone persists in destructive criticism, confront them by naming the problem to their face. *You are trying to put me down. Please don't.* Facing it boldly catches them off–guard, defuses their power. As most bullies are cowards, they will probably retreat from such a show of strength.

Imagine that person who upsets you has grown horns, visible to yourself, or a Pinocchio nose.

Look for the best in that person. Focus on that, and your own less defensive body language and tone of voice will help dissipate tension. Tell yourself:
- It is easier to talk than to do.
- This comment is directed at my performance. It does not belittle my worth as a person.
- This comment refers to my performance today. I played better yesterday and I will probably play better tomorrow. No-one can be brilliant every day.
- I did my best in the circumstances. I will learn from the experience and improve it next time.
- This is just one person's view. Others probably think differently.

Most of us receive useful positive feedback in the course of our studies and careers. Be receptive to this, absorb it. Often, lessons may be hard initially, but reflection later reveals the wisdom behind the words.

Remember how we learned most from a good teacher when we came to lessons with an open mind? (If, however, a teacher consistently destroys confidence and enjoyment with negative, demeaning criticism, it may be time for a change.) If we maintain a receptive attitude, colleagues' suggestions may be very helpful.

Queensland Symphony Orchestra trombonist Jason Redman says:

Be your own best critic—that means no lying about how you do what you do. Admit your weaknesses and faults before others force you to see them, but also remember everything else that is great. We are only as strong as our weakest link know what it is and deal with it, or avoid it if you can't deal with it.

Handling press reviews

A press mention is a major goal and achievement, not only to satisfy the ego, but also to prove one's worth to colleagues.

Critiques are the performing artist's marketing tool, quoted, often out of context, in grant applications, press releases, advertisements and Curricula Vitae. Though primarily the reviewer's words were written for his editor and readers rather than for the performers concerned, they hold a great marketing and economic value for the performers.

Thus the critics' fingers, dancing over their word-processors, hold great powers for good or ill. Are these warranted? Most have heard the saying: 'He who can, does and he who can't, criticises.' When bruised by a scathing review, we instinctively snort, 'Who is he to judge? I bet he couldn't perform as well, let alone better!' We may think that, unlike musicians who may be 'born' with significant talent, critics merely do their job.

Does a critic need qualifications, expertise in music or drama in order to justify his or her opinions? Liszt suggested that reviewers be subject to a system of examinations and licensing. Yet how would one quantify the qualities needed: objective listening, knowledge and understanding of the arts, skilled writing to a deadline?

The critic, like the recording technician, hears and sees a bigger picture than does the performer from within. Dr Samuel Johnson wrote, 'You may scold a carpenter who has made you a bad table, though you cannot make a table. It is not your trade to make tables.' (Scholes, 1970; p. 267)

Some might envy the critic's job. Imagine being paid for the privilege of hearing exceptional performances, sitting in the best seats, when most would be grateful for the back of the stalls. Imagine being considered an expert without having to prove it in front of an audience!

Yet even such opportunities pall. American critic Henry Fink dismissed as 'a bundle of vanity and ambition' a pianist's efforts to impress him with her 'accomplishment.' He wrote (Fink: pp.426-7):

After being a music critic for nearly three decades, I confess that I am deathly tired of concerts and operas and recitals of all descriptions. I long more and more for more expression, but seldom get it...

I long to go among savages and hear them sing their thrilling war songs or listen to their impassioned drum solos. I hate these conservatory pianists with their finicky 'touch' and 'methods'....and technical abominations; I detest those singers of the 'Italian school' whose one idea is to sing notes loud, high and shrill, that will be sure to arouse 'thunders of applause'. Sometimes, I come home from a long recital so hungry for real music that I have to sit down at my Steinway and play a Chopin prelude.

Many critics speak from a genuine wish to raise standards of performance, to stimulate thought and discussion. 'The critic who dares not to attack what is bad is but a half-hearted supporter of what is good,' wrote Robert Schumann. He formed the *Neue Zeitschrift fur Musik* in 1834, so influential that for many years he was better known as a critic than a composer. Through this, he lifted the professionalism of music criticism. Schumann wisely realised that 'the music critic's destiny is to make himself superfluous! The best way to talk about music is to be quiet about it!' He did not inflate the critic's importance: 'Critics always want to know what composers cannot tell them and critics hardly understand a tenth part of what they talk about.' (Walker: p. 200)

George Bernard Shaw, music critic of the London Star and World between 1888 and 1894, sensibly reminded:

A critic should constantly keep his reader in mind of the fact that he is only reading one man's opinion and should take it for what it is worth. (Shaw: p. 268)

However, performers' paranoia might be reinforced by his wry comment: 'Reviewing has one advantage over suicide. In suicide, you take it out on yourself: in reviewing, you take it out on other people.' (Shaw: p. 886)

One thing is certain. A critic does not take on this job in order to win friends, as Hector Berlioz pointed out:

My position as a critic continues to make enemies. And those who hate me most fiercely are not so often those whom I have blamed as those of whom I have not spoken, or have praised faintly. Others will never forget certain pleasantries of mine. . .

The man who hates you is so furious at the praise you are likely to obtain by heartily doing him justice in public, that he detests you all the more, while the man who likes you, not being satisfied with the laboured eulogies you bestow on him, likes you all the less. (Berlioz: p. 484)

Meanwhile, Berlioz complained that it made him sick to have 'to put up with the fawning compliments, meanness and cringing of people who have, or are likely to have, need of you.' (*Ibid*, pp. 217-8)

How critics work

We have probably all heard of newspaper reviews where the critic commented at length on the concert's first half, dismissing the final symphony as 'notable'. And didn't we all see him skulking out the exit just before it began?

It helps to understand the life of a critic. He has probably had to rush away from the concert, foregoing the gossip in the bar afterwards, in order to throw together meaningful analyses of the performance in erudite words to be read over cereal next morning. He has to email it in to the newspaper office by a strict deadline. There is little time to weigh every last word.

Perhaps, we smart that the critic raved over our colleagues and dismissed us with three lukewarm words. Perhaps, our performance did attract glowing words, but the editor saw fit to slash through that whole paragraph with his red pen. Perhaps, he chose to include the few controversial words rather than many tame accolades—after all, controversy sells newspapers! Editors and to some extent the sponsorship of entertainment advertisements decree just how little space arts columns warrant. This often seems a mere token gesture compared with sports pages. From the critic's point of view, it is much harder to write a short than a long review. What should one omit? What most warrants mention?

Brisbane critic Sue Gough indicates the reviewer's dilemma:

The practical aspects of reviewing come down to word counts and content. It is expected that the reviewer will set up and demonstrate some kind of hypothesis, some kind of particular view of the production, within the space of the review. What is it really all about in a cosmic sense? The choice as to where you cut into this particular cake may be difficult. It is also expected that a reviewer will say something about the playwright and his/her previous work, the play's place in the history of drama, the play's plot, structure, character development and social context, the direction, the acting, the design and lighting.

Try this in 600 words. Try it in 400 which is now the norm. Paring back to the word count inevitably involves cutting out those blurring, softening words that provide a safety net for the reviewer: words like 'almost', 'somewhat', 'perhaps'. As a result, I sound much more sure than I really am. And also, as a result, I am further from the truth. There are no absolutes, only balances of probability.

The editor may delete one crucial word to fit space limitations and totally change the original meaning. Canny writers ensure that their critiques are exactly the length specified by the editor, or at least that their most important points are at the beginning.

Many mistakes occur in the chain between the reviewer's pen and the finished critique. Thus, Purcell was said to write *Dildo and Aeneas*, and Offenbach was credited with *All Fierce in the Underworld*. Performers' critiques may also suffer from 'typos', as Brisbane Sunday Mail arts critic Barbara Hebden experienced:

Reviewing a performance of The Marriage of Figaro, I wrote, 'The Countesses' sensitive arias were always beautifully controlled and expressive.' In print, 'arias' was changed to 'areas'.

George Bernard Shaw had similar experiences:

These innocent persons seem to think that whatever appears over my signature in the Star is written by me. This is a mistake. I merely supply a manuscript sketch which the printers fill in according to their own fantasy. I believe I did make some such trite observation as that the mood of the work in question was monotonous. The compositor...altered the word to 'monstrous'. (Shaw: pp. 673-4)

He added that the proofreader, thinking this one of the critic's 'originalities, one of those inspired utterances which distinguish him from the vulgar critic,' displayed it in capitals in a line by itself.

This leads to another important point: that pithy, pungent heading in bold capitals was not written by the reviewer, but by a sub–editor with less interest in cultural matters than in eye–catching titles which would fit the layout. This may have skewed a balanced critique or magnified a small point beyond the critic's intentions.

The function of critics

Before Schumann, the critic's role was to evaluate musical scores, rather than performances, usually in a tolerant, kindly manner in order to mediate and explain matters to the reader. Schumann used his journal to promote new composers while lampooning many established ones, thinly disguised by pseudonyms. However, he saw himself as less a fault–finder than an educator.

From the Romantic era forward, performances were ever more stringently criticised. At least now, our contemporary libel laws protect us from being called 'giftless bastards'. It is unlikely we will be reproached for 'not being brave enough to blow out [our] brains'! (Berlioz: p. 204)

The public tends to read reviews to formulate opinions rather than to decide if an event is worth attending. Except for film, opera and ballet seasons or recordings, many reviews are of one–off events, so a poor review may not affect specific attendances, but more the performer's sense of worth.

The mere word 'critic' is off–putting. Why cannot music and stage reviewers adopt sport's more palatable titles like 'commentators' or 'arts writers'? Their tools of trade –words – to some extent limit positive accolades: how unfortunate that negative adjectives are so numerous and satisfyingly pungent! How easily superlatives can sound excessive or cloying.

How performers have handled criticism

Many performers profess to ignore their critics. Composer–critics have not been noted for their understanding, objectivity or promotion of rival styles. Schumann waged vitriolic warfare on Wagner, Weber attacked Beethoven and Berlioz bitterly resented Cherubini's negative criticism. Wagner called Schubert a 'third–rate talent'. Mozart was described by a colleague, composer Giuseppe Sarti, as 'A barbarian without an ear who has the audacity to write music!'

From the many negative composers' quotes it would seem most have or perceived critics to have rubbed salt into raw flesh:

The worst of musical criticism is that there is so much of it. – Edward Elgar

I had a dream the other day about music critics. They were small and rodent–like with padlocked ears, as if they had stepped out of a painting by Goya. – Igor Stravinsky

Pay no attention to what the critics say; there has never been a statue set up in honour of a critic. - Jean Sibelius

A review, however favourable, can be ridiculous at the same time if the critic lacks average intelligence, as is not seldom the case. – Franz Schubert

Last year, I gave several lectures on 'Intelligence and Musicality in

Animals'. Today, I shall speak to you about 'Intelligence and Musicality in Critics'. The subject is very similar. – Erik Satie

Misbegotten abortions. – Ralph Vaughan Williams.

I have become so used to being slated by those critics that I felt there must be something wrong with me when the worms turned on some praise. – William Walton

Critics love mediocrity. – Giacomo Puccini

[Of criticism:] The most useless occupation in the world. – Giacomo Puccini

I am sitting in the smallest room of my house. I have your review before me. In a moment, it will be behind me. – Max Reger

However, Gustav Holst managed to find stimulus or encouragement from astringent comments:

A sympathetic critic's disapproval is the most interesting and stimulating experience I know... The critical faculty is as important, as necessary, as divine, as the imaginative one: it is impossible to overrate the real critic.

Some performers could afford to mock critics. The pianist Liberace once quipped: 'What you said hurt me very much. I cried all the way to the bank.' Others have been inhibited by negative criticism to the extent of illness or restricted performance. Benjamin Britten's doctor ordered him to cease reading his reviews. Van Clyburn refused to perform in London after savage criticisms from its press. Maria Callas was destroyed by bad critiques. Luciano Pavarotti called the Milanese critics 'sadists', whose hatred might be triggered by reasons unrelated to the performance.

The best way to handle criticism is to use it, to learn from it, to integrate it into one's performance. Violinist Ole Bull turned severe criticism from a Milan journal to his benefit by tackling the critic: 'It is not enough to tell me my faults; you must tell me how to get rid of them.' The critic referred him to a singing teacher and, after six months' wholehearted work, Bull emerged a true artist. (Fink: p. 346)

Virtuoso violinist Louis Spohr admitted to being very annoyed by music director Reichardt's sharp criticism after his first appearance in Berlin. Resentment turned to gratitude when 'I soon found it contained many truths and well–founded strictures and that it had prompted me to correct the faults it pointed out in my execution.' He invited Reichardt to a musical party at his house to hear two new quartets and learned from his comments. (Spohr: p. 125)

Hans von Bulow took a strong reactive stand. He came onstage and remarked that, since the critic had faulted his performance of the *Egmont Overture*, he would not wrong Beethoven again and would instead conduct Brahms' *Festival Overture*. (Schonberg: p. 346)

A common response to criticism is resignation. Schnabel accepts philosophically that 'the critic cannot be criticised for criticising.' (Schnabel: p. 141) Beethoven wrote that, in spite of several faults which he could not prevent, the audience received everything most enthusiastically. Not so the critics (Beethoven letters, p.79):

Nevertheless, scribblers will not fail to write wretched stuff against me in the Musikalische Zeitung... Who troubles about such critics when one sees how the most wretched scribblers are praised by such critics and how they speak in the harshest way of works of art... And now criticise as long as you like, I wish you much pleasure; it may give one a little prick like the sting of a gnat and then it becomes quite a nice little joke.

Horowitz wearily noted that the critics had exhausted their praise and he could not satisfy them whatever he did.

Many performers have cynically noted that two reviews of the same concert can totally contradict each other. Pianist and composer Anton Rubenstein said they were all contradictory: 'They all sound so definite, like judges in a court and yet one says I play too loudly, the other too slow... They wouldn't pardon me a single wrong note and I always play so many.' (Morrison, 1974: p.65)

Critics have been proved wrong! We can take heart from the knowledge that even great artists might have sunk to oblivion if they had allowed judgments from teachers, conservatoria and press to discourage them. Beethoven wept over his early lessons and his music teacher told him, 'As a composer, you are hopeless.' Weber and Wagner were told that they would never amount to much in music. Violinist Joseph Joachim was told he could never become a violinist, while violinist and conductor Louis Spohr went so far as to tell Norwegian violinist Ole Bull he was 'unfitted by nature' to be a musician. (Fink: pp. 404, 409) Caruso's music teacher told him, 'You can't sing; you have no voice at all.'

Polish pianist and composer Ignacy Paderewski lacked confidence because he had no systematic training until twelve years of age. Even more so, because at the Warsaw Conservatoire he was repeatedly told he had no talent and would never make a pianist. (Fink: p. 409) Yet this stiffened his resolve: he was adulated after a brilliant debut, but had to practise insane hours up to seventeen a day to put together enough repertoire to sustain expectations.

What a loss to the world if that most damning word 'mediocre' had daunted both conductor Sir Thomas Beecham and singer Lotte Lehmann; if the latter had taken up a 'practical career' as suggested.

Be grateful for any encouraging critiques you earn and be open to learn objectively from negative or tepid comments. Even the toughest comments may carry useful truths. After all, the critic is not likely to be more wrong when blaming than when praising. German conductor Herbert von Karajan said: 'If you believe the good reviews, you must believe the bad ones, too!' However, remember that any criticism is just one person's opinion, of necessity subjective to some degree. Try to not take reviews too seriously.

One can feel some small sympathy for Berlioz, forced to supplement his precarious income from composition by writing reviews:

But to have to write Feuilletons for one's bread! to write nothings about nothings! to bestow lukewarm praises on insupportable insipidities! to speak one day of a great master and the next of an idiot, with the same gravity, in the same language! to employ one's time, intelligence, courage and patience at this labour with the certainty of not even then being able to serve Art by destroying a few abuses, removing prejudices, enlightening opinion, purifying the public taste and putting men and things in their proper order and place!

Despite Berlioz' despair, he did sum up the positive benefits that a good critic is able to offer to the performing arts. Many excellent critics have in fact made such worthwhile contributions. If we maintain an open mind even in spite of some negative comments, we can improve and mature through criticism (Berlioz: p. 252).

Do reviews matter so much? Hear Bette Midler (Mair: p. 254)

The thing that's satisfying is your relationship with your God, your planet, your family, your friends and how you see beauty and how you see the world. You come down from your perch a little bit... You can't eat your newspaper clippings. And you can't take your newspaper clippings to bed. It's really not that satisfying.

Mime artist Marcel Marceau can have the last word on critics (Martin: 1978):

Critics are sometimes right and sometimes wrong but the great critics are not those who say good things about you, but are those who know about theatre. In time, you sense it. Everybody makes mistakes. As an artist can do good work and bad work, so critics can sometimes be wrong, too.

Never has a critic prevented a great artist from developing and those artists who truly have something to say are able to gain their fame with the help of the critics or in spite of them.

Chapter 27
Retain Students

How long did your students retain their New Year enthusiasm and flourish? Does practice wane as realities of busy lives set in? How many others forge ahead, due to your excellent teaching methods?

Students show varying personalities, abilities and progress, so savvy teachers will vary their approaches. Like my vegetable seedlings, I protect the fragile from the overbearing sun or marauding possums and brush turkeys. Others run rampant like my beans and tomatoes unless directed with stakes. Some, like my spinach, seem to just sit. Frustration can slow my enthusiasm until other gardeners share seeds and success stories. My memories of my own teenage plodding through mistake–riddled practice leads me explore effective practice systems for my students.

Think back: why did Simon/Hannah/Ashley drop out last year? They have talent and ability but their interest fizzled. Why is Amanda's progress slow?

Twenty–first century expectations are that results will happen ASAP, or better still—yesterday! A major difficulty for both child and parent is that progress doesn't happen overnight. What other activity requires regular practice for eventual slow results on the never–never? Soccer, netball and judo only need a couple of sessions per week.

In today's society, music is a rare activity that requires daily input in order to reap results. Those living with a beginner learning a stringed instrument find it especially incomprehensible and frustrating to endure wonky tuning and thin sound.

- Be proactive. Is there a valid reason why Luke doesn't practise? Contact his parents as soon as issues arise, and before your frustration festers. Arrange a time that's convenient for both of you to talk. (*Not* at the end of the lesson while your next student stands on one foot hearing the story of Luke's life.) Perhaps there are family issues; perhaps he has a medical condition such as ADHD; or he really wants to play drums. Communicate early with parents and your year's collaboration will run smoother—and be more productive.
- The transition from primary to high school is a crucial one. There are myriad adjustments, new classes and peers. This is the time when student, parent or both may throw up their hands and drop music into the too–hard basket. Give extra support; make sure they hear the fun ensembles available: the stage band, jazz ensemble, and the orchestra. They play flashier music than did the primary band. Ensembles are the one activity with a vertical mix of students; the players nearby may be prefects who would protect a shy student from playground bullying.
- Hint at the fun to be had at camps and tours. A band, orchestra or music camp is a social activity in which they will meet like–minded friends. (My husband and I met at a music camp and such harmony has forged our relationship.)

Delayed gratification—for teachers

Remember those long journeys with children when we are plagued with repeated 'When do we get there?' So it is with students: we work for results that sometimes seem way off the map.

All students pass through valleys and potholes to reach their peaks. Teachers need past–present–future perspective to remember students' progress thus far while giving them vision for what they can become.

Be heartened that nothing is wasted and they will come through stronger and better people if we support them with wise understanding. The mid–late teen years are tough when many may fall by the wayside, especially if jackbooted–teacher treatment backs overcommitted students into a corner.

How to lose students who are a drain

Do we drag along with students who waste our time and their parents' money with little appreciable progress? In such cases I tell such people it is against my religion to take income from hard-working people whose offspring do not respect the sacrifices they make. If our remonstrance and conniptions do not gain results, try some of these rather drastic steps:

Team up with another teacher and swap bottom-of-the-list students for a month. If they don't return, so be it.

Plan an extended tour or overseas trip and babysit students with a colleague. The downside is financial loss if you discover better students stay there when you return, out of pocket.

Suggest: 'I think you are well suited to drums.' (Or ballet).

List specific areas that must improve with a timeframe, otherwise they should seek another teacher. You have a waiting list and prefer to not turn away keen hard-working customers.

'I'm sorry but I must cut back my hours because I'm pregnant.' This line is not recommended for males. Remember that students come and go but babies will need your time, care and attention for the term of their natural lives, or at least the next few decades.

But you have a contract that says you can terminate lessons, so such dire straits are not necessary.

Chapter 28
When students resist change

The New Year is underway, students are sorted and we draw breath. That sea of fresh faces develops names—and issues. Rhythm–less Richard; double–jointed Dougal; uncoordinated Una; puffed–cheeked Chloe. They struggle if we try to change embedded habits. Many students feel insecure when it is necessary to embark on intensive technical repairs.

What bogey must you tackle before students are free to progress? Rigid bow hold? Scrunched fingers? Slumped posture? The Embouchure Onslaught most challenges me. Whatever your particular technical tangles, consider these points:

Start fresh is easier than start over: it's simpler to cultivate excellent technique and posture in a fresh–faced new student than to take apart and stitch together poor habits. Which students are committed enough to tackle issues? Will they become bored and lose heart on a diet of long notes and slow scales? The slow drip technique may just work in one–on–one tuition, but it is far harder in all–sorts groups, especially of multi–instruments. Do we slow a group lesson of mixed ability for an aspect that is crucial for one student? Meanwhile, the others resist long notes and long to play up–tempo. Must I turn a blind eye and deaf ear to that issue just to keep the group moving?

Consider personality/temperaments

Those of Sanguine or Choleric temperaments may embrace and welcome challenges. The Phlegmatics may resist change out of their comfort zones. Melancholics may feel wounded by perceived criticism. They need encouragement.

Sell the benefits: WIFM (What's in it for me?)

There has to be a reason to change. Give reasons why the effort will be worth it; you will play with a stunning sound; technique will be more nimble. Offer a time estimate: 'With focus you could fix this problem in three weeks and then we will play that piece you like.'

Reassure that others managed similar challenges in so many weeks. Most teachers have had to solve problems in their own technique at some time so can understand the difficulties involved, the ways to tackle them and the worth in doing so. Share your own experiences, the frustrations you felt and your improved facility as a result. We gain rather than lose respect by admitting that we had a similar problem ourselves, but it was worth going through the effort of fixing it to experience greater facility now.

See and hear the difference

Demonstrate exhibit A and B, with elaborate exaggeration:
- Do you hear how pitch improves with a pointy chin?
- The tone is clearer, more focus.
- Do you get sore lips? Blame that embouchure!

Show; don't tell! That's not easy when fixing embouchures. Mirrors can be juggled to catch profile angle. Teachers now carry a useful tool in their pockets—the iPhone camera. It even has video to capture that bouncing chin. First check and follow permission protocols.

Embouchure repairs

This is a saga of crumpled chins, buckled lips and collapsed jaws. Teachers of strings and keyboard may fast–track a few pages.

In the Friday afternoon graveyard lesson slot, the new clarinet teacher, Mr Crotchet, casts an evil eye over Amanda's chin. He pronounces a campaign on her embouchure.

She slinks away, bewildered by talk of pointy chins, tight jaws and stretched lips. After all, her orthodontist hasn't noticed them during two years' tortured appointments.

As the band's lead clarinet and star pupil, Amanda attempts to point her chin during the first of her two practices that week. Then gives up. It seems impossible—and, indeed it is, for her bottom lip is securely pinned inside her mouth by even, orthodontist–shaped bottom teeth and further clamped down by mouthpiece and reed.

Besides, why bother? When she played *The Entertainer* at last term's concert did a crumpled chin stop the audience from applauding?

Next lesson, Mr Crotchet is not impressed. His eye–rolling and sighs escalate as weeks drag into months on a rigid diet of long notes and slow scales. After agony develops into aggro, Amanda escapes onto a baritone sax. Far more cool. Besides, Mr Crotchet is not obsessed about saxophone embouchures—or maybe he is more engrossed in planning his new career in IT.

By the time the replacement teacher, Ms Quaver, takes over, most of the clarinet players are lost to the netball team. Looking for scope through old band photos, she discovers Amanda in the lead clarinet chair. She decides to coerce Amanda back onto her first—and preferred—instrument if she will just adjust that baritone embouchure.

Ms Quaver has endured the ordeal of embouchure–fixing not so long ago at Music College. She remembers that incomprehensible fog in trying to change a habit she cannot see. She knows that fixing an embouchure is the worst phase of insecurity a clarinet student ever faces. She understands that students feel threatened by change.

Ms Quaver plans her battle tactics. She warms up her prey with introductory getting–to–know–you–isn't–this–fun lessons, playing duets. Which enables her to show off her rounded warm tone. There have to be good reasons why Amanda will play better if she changes her embouchure.

'Amanda,' she begins her onslaught conversationally. 'Do you happen to suffer from sore lips? Inside the bottom lip especially?' Amanda does, indeed.

'Aha. I'm not surprised.' Wise nods.

Thinks: now I'll compare chins, like those weight–loss advertisements that show photographs of before–and–after. Ms Q waves an aural carrot before Amanda's ears.

She demonstrates a phrase, played with a grotesque, flabby chin. Asks: How does this sound? Flat? Woozy?

Then Ms Quaver plays the same phrase with her best pointy, stretched chin.

'Which sound and tuning do you prefer?' she asks casually. She rests her case.

Before Amanda has time to sense her tactics or to resist, Ms Quaver throws several everyday, natural ideas at her to locate those crucial 'stretch' muscles:

'Can you whistle?' Amanda can't. 'Never mind. Forget that one.'

She produces a thick shake straw (courtesy of MacDonald's) from her bag. 'Imagine you're drinking through this.' Sometimes this works, but many purse and pucker their lips to drink. Amanda is one of the latter. Never mind. Let's try another tack. Ms Quaver produces a bubble pipe from her bag, instructs Amanda to blow bubbles. Amanda squirms. This is too juvenile.

'Okay, try this one. Imagine how you'd blow a note across a bottle.' Amanda waits for a beer bottle to appear, is disappointed.

'Or have you ever played a note on a flute or trumpet?' Amanda hasn't.

She has just realised that she is enmeshed in the dreaded Embouchure Bivouac. Thinks longingly of her baritone sax. Looks at the clock.

But Ms Quaver retrieves her interest with her *piece de resistance*. She removes her clarinet barrel and blows an unashamed loud raspberry through it.

'Here, you blow on the other end, so we don't share germs. Now you can tell your mother you blew raspberries at your new teacher, hee hee.'

That produces results. Ms Quaver has even more tricks to reinforce her advantage. She prides herself on being cool. She demonstrates chin formation with 'dude' and 'cool'. Mr Crotchet was an 'oo' and 'er' person.

Amanda smiles at her teacher's misguided efforts at hip jargon Ms Quaver pounces. 'See! That's great! Your chin is beautifully stretched. A smile gives you a perfect pointy chin! Easy, isn't it? Just smile. If you overdo it with a grin, the air escapes out the corners of your lips. Clarinet players are fun people. Heh, heh.'

Ms Quaver reaches for the practice notebook to draw profile portraits of her 'before' and a preferred 'after' chin. They discuss which idea clicks for Amanda so she feels the difference between a stretched chin and a collapsed one.

If Amanda can see her pointy chin it will be easier to remember and absorb. Ms Quaver sets up two mirrors at right angles. She scribbles a memo to phone to ask for parental permission to video Amanda with her Smartphone next lesson, and to enlist reinforcement during the week until next lesson. All students feel insecure if they're not sure what to do.

As the bell rings, she tries one last desperate attempt to fix an impression clear enough to last for a week. 'Listen, Amanda, and watch my chin while I play pitch–bends. D'you hear how the pitch sags when my chin does? You can rescue it with your smile muscles. You try. Exaggerate with really gross pitch–bends, have fun with them. Good luck!'

Amanda throws her clarinet in the case, still drippy, and escapes to the relative safety of a Home Economics class. Ms Quaver sighs, thinking, 'I didn't have time to tell her about how to make a habit of it all. Never mind, we'll do that next lesson.'

Chapter 29

Instrument issues

Many excuses for lack of practice feature instruments and equipment. 'Ho hum, here they go again,' teachers sniff. 'Heard it all before.' But wait; perhaps there are some legitimate times we can blame the instrument? Is the student compatible with the instrument? Is it in good repair? Over the years I borrowed several bass clarinets that were in poor condition. Their response was unpredictable, with embarrassing squawks and mishaps beyond my control. I decided I was not a bass player until I borrowed a good instrument and enjoyed the experience of playing it.

Students may be blamed as lazy for minimal practice. Before frustration sours the student–teacher–parent relationship triangle, let's explore some genuine reasons why some students cannot face serious, lengthy and focused work. Teachers may pass on to parents the following considerations before they choose an instrument—or buy it on eBay with no warranty.

Perhaps the problem is not mere lack of motivation. Many abandoned instruments cultivate mould and dust under beds because they were just not suited to their owners.

Size matters

Frustrations can be caused when instruments built for adult–sized hands are put into young children's small fingers. A youngster who lacks fine motor coordination may struggle with a violin but manage a saxophone with ease.

(Imagine the difficulties a small child experiences with a baritone saxophone that is almost bigger than him. Advise him to begin with the alto instrument rather than that tenor or baritone that just happened to be available.) A small trumpeter can start with a cornet, which, being conical, is compact. The weight and finger or arm stretch of tuba, trombone and bassoon daunt smaller physiques. A young girl's clarinet may squeak because her thin fingers can barely cover the holes. She would manage much better with the covered holes of the flute or saxophone.

Playing an inappropriate instrument can cause tension, fatigue and frustration. The worst case is repetitive strain injury. Schools and music shops offer tests to assess a student's suitability to the instrument. Parents should discuss with teachers before reaching for their credit cards.

Many factors come into the equation—the varying rates of physical development, maturity, coordination and concentration. Of course, if a student really loves a particular instrument and its sound, most incompatibility can be overcome.

Many well-intentioned parents begin their children's music lessons before coordination and concentration skills are sufficiently mature. This causes negative impressions: 'Oh, I'm not musical; I gave up the trombone in primary school.' On the other hand, early musical education is to be encouraged. Scientific studies show that music training in the first decades of a child's life increases aural acuity and intelligence, as music uses both right and left hemispheres of the brain.

Early starters

The secret is to choose carefully which form of music is undertaken. Singing, movement and clapping games are ideal from toddler stages. Precursors to playing an instrument are Dalcroze, Orff, Suzuki, Kodály, Colour Strings (a Kodály based string program), Forte, Encore and Yamaha methods. They develop aural, pitch, rhythmic and coordination skills.

The Eurhythmics and Dalcroze Approach was inspired when Emile Jacques-Dalcroze (1865-1950) noticed that a student with poor rhythm walked with natural rhythmic gait. This method integrates rhythm, phrasing and expression through natural and attentive body movement, solfege and improvisation.

The Orff approach is based on 'elemental' music, that is music children make naturally, without training. Speech rhythms and body movements progress to mallet percussion instruments in ostinati, drones and pentatonic melodies. It embraces exploration and experience, listening, physical coordination and improvisation.

Hungarian composer Zoltán Kodály (1882–1967) created a sequenced method to restore his country's musical heritage primarily through singing. This teaches children to read music, improvise and compose, using a movable 'do' solfege (Solfa) with hand signs to represent the syllables do re mi fa so la ti do. The child experiences the 'sound before symbol' concept to develop fluency of pitch, rhythm, form and metre, and at more advanced levels scales, modes and harmonies. (Choksy, 1999)

Keyboard and stringed instruments do benefit from a very young commencement age. It's necessary to solve issues of size, finger stretch and weight with smaller instruments appropriate to the age. Eighth or even sixteenth size violins and celli are available and a three–quarter size guitar.

Don't overlook the human voice as a wonderful instrument; it is free, light and easily transported, unlike the double bass or tuba. It can develop from babyhood on, and offers a repertoire catering to all tastes and styles.

Physical points

Given that young people develop at varying rates, it is important to not take generalisations too seriously. However, the following points are a reasonable rule of thumb:

- Good coordination is required to do justice to the string family. Dr Shinichi Suzuki advocates starting stringed instruments as young as three or four; however, some teachers and parents prefer the benefit of a few years' maturity. Because the viola and double bass require wider hand stretching, it is wise to wait until they may be taken up as a second instrument. As cello and bass are supported on the ground, the weight issue is negligible.
- Most children manage woodwind instruments at approximately aged 10. The bassoon, oboe, tuba or euphonium benefit from waiting until

later years—but there are always exceptions. Some young players cope splendidly.
- Lighter high brass instruments can be played without strain from about nine to 10 years of age. Long–armed year 5 students manage the trombone if they are reasonably well–built. Because of weight, it is advisable to begin with either the tenor trombone or the baritone (three–valve). The F trigger or bass instruments should not be considered until more advanced. Younger players may struggle to reach the sixth and seventh positions on the Bb tenor trombone.
- With lower brass, younger players aged around 10 can begin with single horn or tuba, as they are simpler and lighter than the double instruments. The tuba and all brass in general require solid physical development and more air than for many instruments.
- All brass and woodwind instruments require well–formed dental structure, and it is advisable to begin lessons only when the front adult teeth have stabilised. Playing with gaps caused by lost baby teeth can be tricky. Orthodontic work also may cause discomfort at times but most wind and brass players manage to survive these torrid times. Teachers can suggest a mouth guard to compensate.

If an instrument makes them sick

Complaints like 'my instrument is such poor quality, it gives me a headache to play it' or 'I'll need a better one if I'm going to work harder' may seem mere excuses unless an experienced teacher filters this for parents.

Poor quality equipment can make practice unpleasant, even uncomfortable. Suggest to students that 'there is a better chance that your parents will put their hard–earned money into an upgrade if you have proved motivated and keen.' If they don't play, why should parents pay? They can first expect to see serious effort.

Parents may think it fickle if their children suggest frequent changes of instruments, arguing: 'I think I'd do better with another instrument.' Teachers remind students that it is necessary to give their instruments sufficient time and effort to reap results and satisfaction before giving up. Music isn't a quick–fix game—it's one of the very few fields in our instant–gratification twenty–first century lives that rarely yields immediate results.

Students who wish to learn another instrument while continuing with the present one might save their own money to rent one from a shop, or borrow one from school over the holidays to experiment. They need lessons to set correct foundations and avoid discouragement. Once proficient with one instrument, the next step may seem easy. The ideal match of musician to instrument may take some time to establish. Once compatibility is discovered, the sheer enjoyment of exploring and expressing its wide variety of musical timbres and styles surely creates healthy, disciplined and exceptional young people.

(Adapted from *Practice is a Dirty Word; How to clean up your act* by Ruth Bonetti.)

Chapter 30
Communication and people skills

Sometimes at the end of a long teaching day, I slump on the couch with a wry smile to review my day, and ponder on how my manner changes with different students. With the shy child, my voice is cooing soft; that teenage lad receives bracing briskness. Empathy drips to an adult who lacked confidence. For the parents we adopt professional tones or speak as peers. Some may become good friends over the years.

Let me share with you a Communications Skills In–service: teaching sons to drive. At that age they tell me how my directions come across. I realise that in spite of having the confidence to speak straight to their mother and delivering their commands with the gravitas of their deepened voices, they do admit to insecurities.

'Don't tell me all the things I'm doing wrong, it only makes me less secure.'

'You could have asked if I'm aware what the speed limit is, instead of saying to slow down.'

'Back off; I know what I'm doing!'

Choose which issues are really important and don't overload your students with the small stuff.

Praise works wonders! They're more receptive to hearing the 'Right' than the 'Wrong.' They cherish words that build, rather than belittle, like: 'That was good, you started slowing well before the red light.'

Coping with communication glitches

Music is an international language, but teaching offers communication challenges. Add a foreign language to the equation and there are pitfalls. By Murphy's Law, I discovered this while teaching my very *first* lesson in a foreign language.

When we moved to Sweden so that my husband could lead a Swedish opera orchestra, I didn't know that in time I would also perform with the orchestra. Not one to knit by the (electric) fire, I learned a few phrases of Swedish and phoned the local *Musikskolan* to offer my teaching services. The director answered in unintelligible floods. Blink. *Långsamt, tack.* (Slower, please.) Stig said in careful English that they would welcome my teaching and he would show me the Red Willage.

It transpired that this was a cheerful red—like most north Scandinavian houses—villa in the centre of town. It had airy studios; a library and a kitchen for brewing the many cups of strong coffee that help Swedes function through long winters.

Determined to make this work, I asked a colleague to write down a list of Swedish words I might need: fingers, thumb, breath, tongue, lips, tone, sharp, flat.

My trepidation on meeting the first student relaxed for she was shy but pleasant. She played competently but with little imagination. 'Let's make some interesting dynamics,' I suggested. Swedish children start English lessons at eight years so this fourteen–year–old understood me, even though she was too shy to speak much. 'Do you know what *forte* means,' I asked? '*Ja, ja, fort.*' We tried very fort and not so fort, and not fort at all, with little difference to her musical expression until she departed in polite bewilderment.

It was best for my morale that I only discovered at the end of the day that in Swedish *fort* means *fast*, not loud.

Fortunately, this early experience showed the scope for glitches so I could look out for signals of confusion. Swedish classes soon made the communication effort two–way.

Another incident showed me just how easy communication could fail, even in our mother tongue. I inherited a student from a respected teacher. Dynamic contrasts were unsatisfactory until one day she said: 'Oh, I get it.

You mean this'—sketching a crescendo shape with her hands—'means get louder. And that'—a diminuendo—'means become softer. I always thought it was the other way round.'

Where words fail, music speaks.

– Hans Christian Andersen

Chapter 31
Sell the benefits of learning music

Why do parents invest in their children's music, dance, drama and debating? So others will be impressed by them? To fulfil lost opportunities from parents' own childhood? If so, it would be better if the adults blew the dust off the instruments and played themselves. Or is it to give students a positive experience and vehicle for creative communication and self–expression, so they can set and meet their own goals and challenges?

What do our young children gain from their music experiences? My son at ten years old observed that he found playing long violin bow strokes calming. He had noticed that teenagers who learned music seemed less 'ratty' than others who did not. He accepted the need to practise when he joined school orchestras and enjoyed the sense of fraternity with like–minded peers through rehearsals, tours, music camps, concerts.

The principle that learning to play a musical instrument has a definite civilising effect has been integrated into Japanese education. There, the majority learn violin or another instrument. A major premise of the Suzuki method is that the mother is involved, learning alongside the child. (Suzuki, 1983)

School instrumental ensembles should be a definite priority (time–wise and budget–wise) in schools, for such experiences not only teach teamwork and discipline, but have a civilising effect on participants. Depending on which instruments are played, physical benefits include exercise of large and small muscles, and the development of fine and gross motor coordination. Moving to music exercises body, fingers, lungs and breath control. Intellectually, correlations indicate that music students achieve higher results than non-musical peers.

It has been scientifically shown that listening to classical music by composers such as Mozart and Bach improves brain functioning and hence the overall intelligence.

From her thirty years' teaching experience Melbourne regional instrumental music coordinator, Cheryl Morrow, sums up the benefits for students of playing music:

In its unique way [music] *can offer young people a significant level of support by nurturing self-esteem, self-efficacy and social connectedness. It can also play a major role in the development of important community skills such as leadership, teamwork, patience, persistence and responsibility... In playing a musical instrument not only does a student need to master the physical and technical aspects of learning the instrument, they also need to learn specific listening skills and optimally learn to read musical notation. The aural aspects of learning a musical instrument mirror learning a second language in terms of the listening skills that need to be developed to play stylistically and with appropriate interpretation. Learning to read musical notation is also akin to learning a second language. The black notes and signs on the page need to be intellectually interpreted and communicated to the body in order for the instrument to be physically played, resulting in the production of a recognisable tune.*

In 1975 Venezeula, when Jose Abreu started eleven music students in a garage, it was the genesis of his El Sistema program to offer musical instruments and training to disadvantaged children. Now government funded, it has grown to include 250,000 children playing in 250 orchestras with 50,000 teachers, most of them graduates from the program (at the time to writing, according to SBS documentary Global Village Episode 2545). In this, Abreu advocates the benefits of music for marginalised youngsters in poor neighbourhoods, who learn social skills and to be part of a community. 'Music brings about social change. In the orchestra the children and young people learn what it means to be part of a community. They learn about interdependence, team work, solidarity, and above all, collective enthusiasm for a common goal, a horizon that is above and beyond the community itself.

'I should be dead or in prison by now. That's what happens to people from my background,' says clarinet player and teacher Leonard Costa, who before he encountered El Sistema music as a teenager had been in and out of prison, arrested nine times for drug trafficking and armed robbery. 'You're used to having nothing, nothing at all. Anything you have, it's because you stole it. So when someone gives you an instrument, a tool in fact, that's how I see it, it's like a new door opening, a new chance at life, a chance to grow and learn. Music is such a broad, extensive topic that it becomes part of you. It was so moving for me to receive a clarinet.'

As many students of multicultural backgrounds struggle to integrate while also learning a new tongue, music gives a common language, as Cheryl Morrow describes:

Krystal, a highly intelligent Asian student came to one of the schools I was teaching at as a shy and withdrawn student. She was finding it hard to fit into the school environment and was struggling with the language... Krystal struggled initially to fit into the music program environment but she was among students who had a common language with her in music, and her evident skills engendered a lot of respect from them. Due to the smaller and more informal learning music program environment Krystal began to gradually form friendships whilst she had struggled in the wider school community. At the conclusion of her first school year she was laughing and joking around with students in the band and had developed some strong connections. Her social confidence blossomed in the music environment and according to feedback from colleagues, the effects flowed across into all other areas of her school life.

21st Century technology has added to the usual pressures of adolescence the prevalence of cyber bullying and cyber predators. Cheryl Morrow writes of the benefits of a music program to combat this: 'Experience has demonstrated to me that this type of behaviour in schools primarily occurs in the student's immediate peer group environment. Involvement in instrumental music programs where students often socialise with a wide range of students across different year levels can provide a haven for students who are being socially excluded or bullied.'

Cheryl describes the experience of Amber who joined the instrumental music program and quickly progressed on her instrument.

She was enthusiastic and loved being part of the band at school. However in her immediate peer group she was being ostracised and sometimes bullied for unknown reasons. Although this was being addressed by the school Amber was often miserable and lonely, particularly during lunch breaks. As Amber became more integrated into the instrumental music program she began to form new friendships with other students in the program. During lunch breaks she would often visit the music department with her new friends and they would book a music room to practice together. Amber began to take on a new cheerful disposition and her work in other subjects began to improve. Being involved in the instrumental music program at school helped Amber to not only to survive a painful social period in her school life, but also to feel more connected at school and improve in her schoolwork in general.

✧

Research by the Australian Music Therapy Association provides some fascinating insight into the impact of music on the human body, as it looks at the links between music–making and physical, emotional and spiritual wellbeing, from womb to tomb.

- A baby's brain is wired for music while in the womb. The musicality of the mother's voice creates an immediate and powerful bond and is pivotal to the infant's survival.
- Learning a musical instrument makes a positive impact on most aspects of a child's development.
- It can also be particularly helpful in remedial learning for dyslexic children. Asthmatic children gain breath control and capacity by playing wind and brass instruments.
- Making music is a positive expression for adolescents.
- Music making can help in alleviating depression and reducing anxiety and can help to encourage a positive attitude.
- Familiar songs retain a place in our memory right to the end of life. People with dementia can benefit from music.

See: www.makingmusicbeingwell.org.au

Stay up to date with current research about the benefits of music at websites such as: http://blogs.scientificamerican.com/science-sushi/2012/08/21/even-a-few-years-of-music-training-benefits-the-brain/
http://www.nature.com/neuro/journal/v10/n4/abs/nn1872.html
http://www.pbs.org/parents/education/music-arts/the-benefits-of-music-education/
http://www.musetude.com/

✦

Noise pollution is an irritant in our world. Imagine the lowered stress in our world if we could persuade supermarkets and public facilities to play real music instead of musak! Calming or uplfting; relaxing or upbeat, but not brain-numbing. A culture-shocked Stravinsky is said to have attacked a Hollywood supermarket's sound system with a screwdriver.

Chapter 32
Special needs students

My first reaction was cautious: what can I add to the difficult equation of teaching students with learning difficulties? Then I considered my current experience with one and the challenge it brings me. My best efforts were to enlist parental involvement and listen to the student. Above all, to be flexible in expectations.

Never underestimate the value of music education to special needs students. All are different and respond in varied ways. Those who teach students with ADHD, ADD, dyslexia or Aspergers need to be aware that these are not disorders but the way they process information. Be flexible. Some may experience sensory overload; therefore be prepared to back off it becomes too much for them. Teaching is never a simple process and we can encounter unexpected pitfalls all the more with special needs students.

The following behaviors are often associated with Asperger syndrome.
- Limited or inappropriate social interactions.
- Robotic or repetitive speech.
- Challenges with nonverbal communication (gestures, facial expression, etc) coupled with average to above average verbal skills.
- Tendency to discuss self rather than others.
- Inability to understand social/emotional issues or nonliteral phrases.
- Lack of eye contact or reciprocal conversation.

- Obsession with specific, often unusual, topics.
- One-sided conversations.
- Awkward movements and/or mannerisms.

✧

Communicate with parents—advice that would have helped me better handle an experience years ago. As I tried to drag rhythm and notes from a disinterested teenage boy, his mother's voice erupted from the couch:

'You haven't said a positive thing to the poor kid all lesson! How do you *expect* him to improve?' Thinking back later, I decided this was not valid. I rang the mother and suggested that her son would respond better if she waited out in the car. It was only then that I discovered his ADHD. Mother Dragon huffed and puffed, but opted to take her car and son elsewhere. It was a nasty experience, but looking back, it's clear that the boy's learning deficiencies and reluctances compounded an incompatibility to the instrument. The situation would have been avoided if the parent had told me earlier of his learning difficulties. (See earlier under Agreement.) Team with the parent and other teachers to ask with discretion how they best draw out the often-exceptional talents.

Without such information, or if the child is not diagnosed we may struggle in the dark, suspecting issues but not sure how to tackle them. The key features associated with symptoms of inattention associated with ADHD include:

- Difficulty sustaining attention in tasks or play.
- Not listening when spoken to.
- Not following through on instructions and failure to finish tasks.
- Difficulty organising tasks and activities.
- Avoiding, disliking or being reluctant to engage in tasks that require sustained mental effort.
- Losing things necessary for tasks or activities.
- Easily distracted.

The key features associated with symptoms of hyperactivity (sometimes known as hyperactivity-impulsivity) include:

- Fidgeting and squirming in seat.
- Leaving seat when expected to remain seated.

- Excessive running about or climbing.
- Difficulty engaging in leisure activities; often 'on the go'.
- Talking excessively or blurting out answers before a question is completed.
- Interrupting others.

My next attempt to teach a child with special needs is still a work in progress but has the advantage of a close rapport with the parent. Issues had been apparent long before Aspergers ADHD was confirmed–as the end of year concert. He played well in an accomplished trio but when his solo Gigue was announced flew into a frenzy and stopped mid-way. He was persuaded to finish it, but then threw his instrument into his case and stormed off. The problem? He was so focused on the trio that he did not register he would perform a solo as well. Even though this was clearly written in his journal, he had performed the Gigue for a competition and an exam and had rehearsed it with the accompanist in the weeks before. It was something of a relief for all to hear the diagnosis.

I phoned John's mother to ask 'How can I bring out the best in your child? Am I doing right? What am I doing wrong?'

From such a phone call I learned:
- Be structured.
- Be predictable: no sudden surprises.
- Be explicit with instructions and keep them simple.
- Be definite: 'This is what we will do; this is how it's going to be.'
- But be prepared to negotiate.
- Allow time for processing and response.
- Model for the student to imitate.
- Give opportunities for repetition and practice.
- Run to time.
- Tick off boxes for 'This is what we want to achieve.'
- No two students are the same in their responses.

With students of varied needs I start the lessons with some Brain Gym concepts: a drink of water, a few minutes cross–crawl, 'brain buttons' (massage of collar bone while holding the navel) and positive points (see earlier). Thus, I put together and emailed a schedule in advance:

John's Lesson Plan
Bring to lesson:
Journal [ ] *Enjoy Playing the Clarinet* [ ] Orchestra music [ ] Water bottle [ ]
Drink some water
Do cross–crawl for 2 minutes
Put instrument together.
Play long notes x 3 (8–10 seconds each)
'Positive points'—hand on forehead and slow deep breaths.
Play *Gorilla Jumps*—half a page.
Play page 26 *Enjoy Playing*, top line.
Play scales: F major 2 octaves: C major 1 octave.
Drunken Sailor (for eisteddfod)
- Clap and count rhythms
- Say aloud and finger notes in the rhythms—section 1.
- Play chromatic scale 2 octaves.
- Say aloud and finger notes in the rhythms—section 2.
- Say aloud and finger notes in the rhythms—section 3.
- Play all through slowly.

My anticipations of a breakthrough with John were dashed. In my efforts to provide predictable structure, I overlooked the advice that unexpected changes could throw him off balance. They did. At the next lesson he could not play at all. He announced he would give up playing.

I fixed the instrument mechanism (he often expressed his frustration by thwacking the instrument) and adjusted the reed. We turned back to earlier pages for the register crossing that he has baulked at for several years. I back-pedalled on pressure of an eisteddfod. Played a fun duet then said 'See you next week.' No, he vowed, 'I'm giving up.'

After discussions with his mother I planned three-point tactics for next lesson when he would come 'just for a chat' to tell me of his timetable and academic pressure.
- 'Scientific research shows that those who play music tend to excel with their academic studies as a result.' Faint interest.
- 'It's orchestra policy that members must have lessons. You were

awarded a bronze medal last year for your participation. This year might be silver.'
- 'School policy is that students must give a half term's notice. Rather than forfeit this outlay, we could play some easy pieces. I'll accompany you on piano and we record them so you can go out on a high with a CD of '*John's Greatest Hits.*' Your grandparents will love that as a Christmas present.'

I offered easy new pieces that were short, accessible and mostly low register. Even though he has been recorded playing upper notes, this is a mental block for him, so I desisted. It was a scatty lesson as he had not taken his medication that morning and literally climbed the walls to pull down posters and replace them sideways. But his overall manner was positive and he departed with five albums to consider 'just until mid-term.' Even, he remembered to pick up his instrument before the end of the day. The next week he was more focused and we played through some new pieces. He welcomed my interest in his condition, discussed openly how it affects him and nominated an alias for this account.

We are still moving forward, if slowly. He may be hesitant in many aspects but plays pieces with beautiful musical expression.

One student I have taught with Aspergers was quite brilliant on clarinet and high-performing. However this student occasionally had temperamental outbursts, writes Cheryl Morrow. *Once after having played a duet in a competition she stormed off stage voicing a loud opinion on how unsatisfactory the performance had been. I can also recall a musically brilliant percussion student with Aspergers. The only clue to this student's Aspergers was occasional hypersensitivity. He took everything very seriously. However he was an absolute pleasure to teach as apart from impeccable manners. The student worked very hard and managed to master the most difficult percussion parts.*

My own lessons have been to develop patience, flexibility and to use much positive reinforcement. To hearten us all, I forwarded an internet link to his mother of examples of genius who might have been diagnosed as Aspergers ADHD if it were known in their day.

While retrospective diagnosis is flimsy, my search located the following who may have experienced some form of the autism spectrum: Mozart, Beethoven, Albert Einstein, Charles Darwin, Isaac Newton, and Michelangelo. That might encourage those students who struggle with low self-esteem and an inability to fit square pegs into round holes. Many may outgrow some disabilities such as ADHD or ADD as they mature. Useful information is at http://musicmattersblog.com/category/teaching–ideas/teaching–special–needs–students

This site quotes Susan Barton, founder of the Barton Reading and Spelling System, based on the Orton–Gillingham Multisensory Method:

Children with dyslexia have a different brain structure. Their right hemisphere is actually larger than most people's, and they have different nerve pathways in the language processing part of their brain. And I love to share with people that their right hemisphere is larger than most people's, because it explains why they're so gifted in skills controlled by the right side of their brain. So yes they struggle with reading, writing, spelling, but they'll be better than their peers in either artistic ability, athletic ability, music, mechanical ability... Superb three–dimensional visual–spatial skills, a vivid imagination, an incredibly accurate sense of intuition. And the most creative, global thinkers you've ever seen.

Students with physical disabilities can relate to DVDs of Violinist Itzhak Perlman and bass-baritone Thomas Quasthoff. Accomplished blind musicians include Andrea Boccelli, Ray Charles, Stevie Wonder and George Shearing.

Inspiring percussionist Evelyn Glennie is deaf, yet she has called her 'disability' a gift from God! 'I can hear music on a level which no-one else can – I hear music with my whole body.' She says: 'Except for a few minor inconveniences, I am not disabled from achieving anything in my career or private life. How then do the terms "Disabled" or "Deaf" really apply to me? In short, they don't, not even the "Hearing Impaired" label works because in some respects my hearing is superior to the average non-impaired person. I simply hear in a different way to most people.'

It's all a matter of attitude.

'I have had a hearing impaired student who managed very well with a very good hearing aid.' Cheryl Morrow writes. 'He was an excellent student;

producing a good tone, and doing plenty of practice.'

There will be times when we take three steps back in our teaching, but rest assured that our efforts make significant impact for good in their lives. Brisbane piano and reeds teacher, Julie Price, describes how she used technology to help such a student:

I reckon I saved this child's life – a grand statement, perhaps, but true. She had a lot of problems and was very dysfunctional socially and emotionally. She had some real physical impairments like serious heart problems so she had spent a lot of time being the weak one; she had been shifted around between families so was totally disconnected from a lot of things. She started to talk to me about some of that but said 'please don't tell my mother.'

I decided the best way to help her musically was to give her an opportunity on piano, so we did creative play with keyboard and computer. We would think of a little motif and she'd make up abstract stories, sometimes like dreams. That was easier to manage, as I didn't have to talk with her about issues too much. She would keep bringing them up and we'd create abstract music, different effects on the keyboard that layered on the free Audacity site. I saved them in a file, and some of them she named strangely. I recorded the quieter, peaceful ones and she took them home on a disc so she could listen to it and relive the story. 'We did some things about her feelings today,' I told her mother.

Chapter 33
The gifted student

Teachers and parents of a potential prodigy face unique opportunities to guide and to find the right proportion of challenge or overstretch. The term 'prodigy' is used here for one who at aged ten or thereabouts performs at the level of a talented adult. The gifted child is one whose level is about one-third higher than contemporaries.

Wouldn't we teachers do all in our power to nurture genius if it appeared in our midst? But there are many pitfalls both for the gifted and those responsible for their care, as we shall see from experiences of famous prodigies.

What do talented young players need in order to flourish, to develop their exceptional abilities to the full? They do thrive on challenges. As government haggles over funding models to lift the standard of education to world-class levels, they should give more attention to the many gifted and talented students who loll through classes and syllabi that offer little for their capabilities and intelligence.

But teachers and parents walk a tightrope to assess whether robust demands may be too much for their relative immaturity to handle. Whether too much focus on their skills is to the detriment of a balanced lifestyle. They must develop as people, socially, mentally, physically, rather than the bulk of their days linked to their instrument by an invisible umbilical cord. They need to experience life in order to project its humanity. Gifted people often excel in several fields. Involve and expose them to other art forms, to express the richness of life and society. Above all, they must enjoy their childhood, for their talent will often lead them to play adult 'games' on adult terms.

Pressure to maintain standards means long hours' daily practice at the expense of normal social life. They face stresses from which most adults flinch. Support from teachers and parents can alleviate or prevent burnout.

Many prodigies fade after a few hectic years unless allowed to develop without undue stress, at a livable pace while still rising to challenges. Some give up, others move sideways to other fruitful paths, some go on to productive, long careers. What factors differ?

The proportion of prodigies who struggle through to adulthood is low; emotional and physical burnout is common. Of the forty-four child prodigies documented in the (London) Musical Times between 1844 and 1944, only eight were still famous as adults. (Lim: 1994: p.10)

Would the others have fared better if their parents had the wisdom of Pablo Casals' mother? She believed that what will be will come in its proper time and in its natural way. If she had allowed Pablo's exploitation by taking the boy to London to likely prominence earlier, he could have been a *Wunderkind*. He might have been displayed 'half as prodigy and half as sideshow attraction in a short-pants velvet suit and white sailor collar'. No doubt it was from his mother that Casals learned that 'only the mediocre are impatient the great know how to wait'. (Kirk: p.66)

In spite of his mother's unfailing support, the young Pablo would not earlier have had the emotional strength to cope with the demands of an international career. His mother's wisdom allowed him to develop at a manageable pace, to the extent that he maintained a significant career up until his death at ninety-seven. A sensitive person, he fought agonising nerves before performances. But these could not quench his love of music, of people and of life. How long might his career have lasted without the wise guidance of his mother?

Some might have been 'prodigies' if treated as such. Pianist Alexis Weissenberg occasionally played in public as a child, but was never exploited. He said, 'You are only a child prodigy if your parents treat you as such.' (Duval: p. 332)

Pianist Alicia de Larrocha insisted she be given piano studies at three.

This child prodigy was never forced onstage as her mother and aunt, both exceptional pianists, understood the marketplace:

> The only thing they cared about was that I loved music and that it was my life. They were happy because I was happy. They never thought about concerts, but little by little I started, just as a test, once a year before a small audience. We never, never thought about it from the point of view of money- even though the family was not well off. In the beginning, I always played for nothing.

Her advice to parents of talented children is, 'If the child is really gifted, encourage him to work as much as possible, to love what he is doing and forget about the career. If it comes, it comes.' (Duval: p.135-6)

How teacher-parents guided prodigy children

Leopold Mozart was an exacting, critical pedagogue and author of a respected violin method. His position as Salzburg Vice-Kapellmeister interested him less than furthering the career of his son Wolfgang. His life was packed as teacher, entrepreneur, organiser and courier. To tour Europe with his wife and two children was a feat in the 1760s.

When Wolfgang asserted independence it is no surprise that he was estranged from his father. He escaped Leopold's dominion and safe Salzburg employment for dubious career prospects in Vienna. Would Leopold have approved of any girlfriend or wife who caught Wolfgang's eye? When Wolfgang married Constanze, Leopold described himself as a victim with 'no choice' but to give his blessing.

Leopold died a lonely man and Wolfgang's brilliant prospects fizzled to a pauper's grave at thirty-six. Would he have fared better in safe Salzburg under his father's wing? The father-son relationship was a complex one; Leopold was shrewd and wise enough to establish his son's career. His flaw was an inability to go of the older Wolfgang.

Rites of passage through adolescence towards adulthood are crucial times for all. Exceptional talents have an added issue. The prodigies who shone as children may feel beached on plateaux in their teenage years, while peers catch up and overtake them. Another insecurity of this time is whether the public may tire of them. At twenty, after twelve years in the spotlight, pianist

Daniel Barenboim found audiences less interested, although he won back their respect as a mature performer.

Casals later described his 'epoch of distress' which lasted a long time and made him physically ill. Around his sixteenth birthday, his depression was so intense that he was obsessed with the idea of suicide.

Teachers and parents of the talented may exert wise, positive influence in the formative years, then come into conflict when the child grows and exerts independence. Thus the doting father, Leopold Mozart, came close to breaking his son's spirit as the love-hate relationship led to resentment and frustration. Wolfgang complained that his father treated him as if he were an archscoundrel or a blockhead or both and he had trouble and worry enough without unpleasant letters. . . 'Do trust me always, for indeed I deserve it.' (Mozart *Letters*: p.160)

Clara Wieck was raised by her father, teacher and mentor, Friedrich Wieck with the express intention of making her a great pianist. He succeeded through his regime of discipline, hard work and his own teaching principles.

With such single-minded expectations, her life was rigidly organised for music. Clara wistfully said later that her father never allowed her to read. Yet Wieck was too good a teacher to overwork her and, as a child, Clara practised only two hours a day. Although she performed throughout Europe from a young age, Wieck could not be acused of outright exploitation. (Schonberg: p. 224) Their relationship foundered when she grew older and wanted to marry composer Robert Schumann.

Any marriage would have been anathema in Wieck's eyes, for Clara was to be a pianist, not a *Hausfrau*. The couple won after intense, vitriolic legal battles. Wieck was bitter to lose his star pupil, who boosted both his ego and bank account. In the process he was estranged from his daughter and became a vindictive, petty and irrational man.

Early training proved invaluable, for both Mozart and Clara Schumann remained creative musicians until their deaths. Clara raised a large family, supported a mentally ill husband, was the first female professor in the Frankfurt conservatorium, and was a significant teacher and performer. However, these examples reveal that adolescence proves a significant stage in prodigies' development.

The crucial adolescent years

Adolescence, from the mid-teen years to early adulthood, forms a critical Rubicon which all gifted performers must cross if they are to continue development as significant adults.

Also a child prodigy, Claudio Arrau observed (Duval: p.19):

So many child prodigies get stuck at a certain moment in their development, the moment of transition from intuitive to conscious playing. That's the dangerous time. From a very early age, I felt a sense of responsibility to the piano, to the works I was playing. If something went wrong, I blamed myself for it. I was very severe with myself even though I was only a child.

Teachers can use tact to help loving, well-meaning parents loosen their influence as a child grows to adolescence. The film, *Shine*, tells of a father's detrimental pressure on Australian pianist David Helfgott. His father's wish that he perform the mammoth Rachmaninov third concerto in his Albert Hall debut resulted in a brilliant performance – then collapse. Helfgott spent twelve years in mental institutions, cut off from both the parent who had disowned him and from the piano which had been his whole life. His return to the concert platform is an inspiring true story of redemption by love, sustained by the encouragement and constant care of his wife. Yet he did not reach the potential he might have realised.

One conclusion can be drawn in the complex issue of teaching and raising gifted children. Burn-out appears to occur less in those prodigies blessed with wise, supportive teachers and relaxed parents. Pianist Pamela Page was a prodigy who picked out Schubert melodies on the piano at two years, but her family took her away from a more demanding teacher because 'they wanted me to have a normal childhood'.

In turn, after she married fellow pianist Max Olding, their son Dene was not forced into a career as violinist. On the contrary. His mother continues:

As a boy, Dene was interested in cricket and astronomy, and he would say that two musicians were enough for one family. He played the violin quite well, considering he only practised ten minutes a day! Then at aged twelve, he began to work more seriously. When he won a competition, he started to think, maybe this is for me.

We were unsure what to do, but when Max was in the USA on a Churchill

Fellowship and sabbatical, we took Dene to play to several teachers to get a couple of opinions. He was accepted into the Julliard School and the decision was made for us. We agonised over sending him there at fourteen years of age. It was a big wrench to be separated from him, with his parents back in Australia, but we just wanted him to make his own way.

That way took him to positions as concertmaster of the Sydney Symphony Orchestra, of the Australian Chamber Orchestra and with the Australia Ensemble.

It is normal for teenagers to search for identity and to test limits. Young children are generally happy to please their parents and teachers, to carry out their wishes as best they can, especially if their relationships are positive. In the intermediate ages, they must learn to be more self-reliant. A nurturing relationship becomes stifling if teachers and parents cannot adjust to this change. If children do not learn to think and feel for themselves now, they may never do so.

If performers are not allowed to explore their self-dependence, as opposed to dependence, an inner tension is created between them and the opposing force, the authority figure. This can create physical spasm and continual insecurity. Like Pavlov's dogs, the repetition of such experiences would implant on their mind the memory bank of tension, causing a ripple effect. In later life, merely facing an authority figure such as a conductor may trigger a wash of subconscious memories and reactions. It is not surprising that those of whom much is expected must require especially supportive rather than destructive parents to nurture them through the crises of confidence and focus.

James Cuddeford, violinist and composer, says:

The progression from unconscious to conscious playing can be extremely difficult for a young musician. It is extremely important at this transition period for parents, teachers, colleagues and agents to be sensitive. Give room and space for the growing musician to develop at his own pace. A great teacher will, during these years, help the student progress from being taught to self-teaching. I have been lucky to be aware enough of my own development from instinctual to controlled playing. My teachers have never imposed outside, artificial intelligence onto my own developing one.

James' parents made enormous sacrifices to allow him and his cellist sister Tara to develop their talent while allowing them to develop at their own will. His mother Dillys said:

I never listened to classical music until James started playing it, though now I love it. Not being musicians ourselves, we only realised he had talent when his primary school music teacher told us he had perfect pitch (I didn't even know then what that meant!) and that we should buy him a violin. That was at age seven, and he progressed so fast that she had the sense to advise us nine months later to send him to a specialist teacher.

He was so keen and dedicated that we didn't need to push. He and Tara would set their alarm, get themselves up at 4.30 a.m. to practise—we didn't tell them to. Then they were fortunate to go to a musical school so they didn't have to battle with peer pressure to conform, like 'Why don't you play soccer?' And sure, it was a sacrifice for my husband to give up his job when we took them to England to the Menuhin School, but they loved it there. I don't know anything about burnout. We just let him go at his own pace, never pushed him.

Exploitation of talented children could be labelled child abuse in some cases. Many childhoods have been stunted in the name of art or for the parents' financial gain. Genius is a tough master.

After Franz Liszt turned his back on a brilliant stage career, he dissuaded a mother from pushing her son too early, confiding: 'You cannot imagine how it spoils one to have been a child prodigy.' He was exposed to public criticism as a prodigy, long before he was prepared to meet the inevitable consequences of public appearance. 'This was an incalculable injury to me. Let this child be spared such a fate.' (Fink: p. 353)

Mendelssohn was a prodigy who gained high respect as an adult. He advised the guardians of violinist Joseph Joachim to allow the boy some years' rest from public life during which he could study, not only music, but science and other areas that would broaden his education: 'He should develop both mind and body with walking and rest.'

This aspect is important. Many brilliant musicians are equally talented in other fields, such as mathematics. They need a balance of stimulus from other fields in order to develop as rounded personalities. They need to enjoy the wealth of challenge and stimulus of the wide world, of other art forms.

The life of the prodigy is not easy. Any performer's ability to cope with pressure can be helped by understanding from positive teachers and parents. Those reared in an atmosphere of controlling, critical, ambitious expectations may flounder. Parents who tend to restrict the expression of emotions can inhibit the communication so necessary to perform. Some children receive little praise for fear they may 'get a swollen head'.

It is possible to survive, even thrive in spite of the struggles prodigies face. Pablo Casals still inspired his listeners with the warmth and depth of his conducting and cello-playing in his nineties.

Artur Rubenstein, prodigy at ten, enjoyed a long and brilliant career. His playing was so exquisite that audiences barely noticed his notorious mistakes. He did not let them inhibit himself. His secret lay in a lack of technical obsession, his enjoyment of his life and music. It is significant that Rubenstein described himself as the 'happiest man I know'. (Morrison: p. 65)

Part 3

TEACHER – PARENT

Chapter 34
Positive Parent Relations

Positive parental involvement is a secret weapon that helps their offspring to progress. Enlist them to the cause of their child's music success and bring them onside. Extol the benefits of learning music. 'All children everywhere,' wrote Dr Suzuki in his book *Nurtured by Love*, 'are brought up by a perfect educational method—their mother tongue. Why not apply this to other faculties?' The parent is the cornerstone of the Suzuki triangle of teacher, student and parent, and learns the instrument along with the child. He says: 'Parents who understand children make fine teachers. An unlimited amount of ability can develop when parent and child are having fun together.' (Suzuki:1983). Create a 'Power of 3' triumvirate of student–teacher–parent to divert parents from unhelpful demands into positive reinforcement. Sometimes these can be part of the problem.

Zealous parents

If we harness the zeal of well–meaning parents they can support regular home practice. They can listen to scales and initiate charts to list practice times. They'll find the scale book hidden behind the piano. They'll motivate their offspring to play concerts and examinations.

When it comes to exams and competitions, however, they can often be more of a hindrance than help. A common complaint is: 'My parents get so uptight about each performance.' Parents can spread tension like a virus through the warm-up room. It's enough stress for young performers to manage the performance without an embarrassing drama as well.

Being a mother has made me a more tolerant, realistic teacher—especially with students who struggle with expectations from all sides in their final high school years. I understand performance stress. I also relate to parent competition stress. The most level-headed parent may become frazzled from organising extra lessons, accompanists and their rehearsals and photocopies for the adjudicator. Then they must locate far-flung Eisteddfod venues in time for the warm-up. However, if you feel that your students' parents create excess stress, try this line:

'I think your son/daughter will manage this better if you give them space to focus.' Then pass them the newspaper and wave them towards the foyer.

Parents expect results

There they are, juggling the driving and funding for multiple after-school activities in hectic lives. If the budget tightens, they may axe any area where they don't perceive their child achieves results. How do parents measure 'success'?

Compare music lessons with sport; teams count their wins and losses across the season, they tally up their progress to zone, state and national finals. The swimming squad records the times of their laps down to milliseconds each week. They bring home a magic number that is a nanosecond faster than last week's. How boring is that, up and down a pool, compared with a Bach fugue? But the parent sees progress. How can we send back a weekly score? How do they gauge music success if all teachers offer is: 'Here's a sticker. Keep up the practice. How about a concert or exam at the end of the year?'

Parents value regular feedback through verbal communication (face to face, by phone, or email). Most notice stickers in the notebook or award certificates that praise any small improvement. Writing regular notes to the parent can ensure that the lesson journal is opened from one week to the next. In my practice journal *Practice WAS a Dirty Word: Music journal* I give parents ownership, with space to list their own goals and comments.

As our world becomes increasingly litigious, many music teachers feel under threat from their 'employers'—parents of students. Other parents abuse our time, take our services for granted and are co-dependents when their children baulk at practice. In a user-pays society, there is an increasing concept that teachers must meet parental expectations. Would we match the teacher's forbearance in this YouTube clip http://www.youtube.com/watch?v=uDF3CHqqb-4&feature=youtube_gdata_player

A colleague was served notice for 'harassing' a nine-year old music student. Granted, the media has cited dire cases of actual abuse, but this person is a pleasantly spoken, diplomatic music teacher known for bringing out the best in her students. Her crime? Following school policy, she went to the child's class to remind her—yet again—it was time for her music lesson.

We teachers need to learn ways to assert ourselves, to set boundaries in order to use our gifts and training for the best results. Then we can continue to enjoy our teaching as a valuable profession, which enriches and changes the lives we contact.

Learn to set boundaries

In my early teaching days, before I learned this important tool, I passed on a model student. She was a dream to teach. Intelligent, a conscientious worker, she produced a positive sound. She played scales daily. An A for her seventh grade exam was likely. The reason? I had an allergy to her formidable mother and her intrusive habits. She would phone during Sunday afternoon siesta, asking to reschedule the next day's lesson to accommodate their social life. Or to fret about whether her dutiful daughter worked hard enough.

There was a *tsunami* when I broke the news that I was downsizing my hours and could not continue to teach her daughter. The pleas were heartrending: it was most inconvenient, she was soon to audition for tertiary institutions, how could I possibly desert her? Once the cyclone subsided, I was free. It was the *best* decision. No longer did I dread Thursdays at 5pm. Since then, I have learned the far better course—to set boundaries with parents and students, and prevent such dire straits.

Should parents sit in on lessons?

There are parents and there are parents. Most are delightful people, supportive, caring. Many will become lifelong friends. If the child is comfortable to have a mother or father in the room, welcome them. They will reinforce the practice. Young children, and shy ones, relax with a parent's moral support so close at hand.

Other parents sit on the couch reading a book, but inhibit their child with their pugilist body language, interjections and hisses. Tight–lipped, shoulders squared, no need for words—until the drive home. The child plays all the notes in the right time, the right place, but with little flow or expression.

Let us meet some of the various categories of *parentus genus*:

Pushy parents

It is inevitable that parents compare their child with others. If Millie gained her letters at age 14, so should Mandy. Never mind that she is not mature enough or would have to jump four grades to do so. Or that she does a fraction of the practice required for a professional level of assessment. Those who fast track the exams miss much important development and wonderful repertoire. Attempts to overreach students' ability set them up for failure and a resulting loss of self–esteem. Living up to school culture can cause one-upmanship, especially in high-achieving colleges.

Proud parents

See above for tactics to support the gifted student. Teachers encounter a tricky equation when trying to work with the 'my child is a genius' fallacy. Some doting parents push their children to higher levels than they can cope with.

'My father seems to think I'm going to be a musical prodigy. I just want to be a computer programmer.'

Warn such parents of the dangers of burnout. Cite the pianist Franz Liszt. This megastar became 'weary of the public, weary of their cheap applause.' For the last 40 years of his life he gave only charity concerts.

The high–flyer parent

These will pay whatever it takes for lessons, top quality instruments, music and equipment. Having done so, they deserve results, even if the child does not contribute any effort to the equation. If they are disappointed, it may be the fault of the teacher. They heard on tuckshop duty that Ms Quaver is the best in the state and so check her availability.

Who is this for? People want their children to have wonderful opportunities that they missed themselves. Fine. If they try to realise their own dreams through your students, perhaps they could take lessons also. Tell them that it is never too late. What they lack in finger dexterity can be balanced by their maturity and motivation.

The low–flyer parent

I just want my child to have fun. 'My children are talented but all that practice causes stress. We just want them to enjoy their music.' Such parents protect their children from the necessary pain thresholds of challenging work. How else will the student manage that favourite piece of music? They don't realise that the frustration of meagre technique will diminish any enjoyment.

The students know how the music should sound, for they've heard it on CD or iTunes; their inferior version only lowers their self–esteem. Odd, isn't it, that parents support hours, days, and seasons of sports practice without similar qualms?

Parents who want their children to 'enjoy' music and improve without practice must understand that without effort there will be no progress and therefore no personal satisfaction.

Try these lines:

'Ah, Mr Floosis, remember how we didn't like consistent work as youngsters and now we look back with pride on our progress. At least your son gains more from his practice time than by playing violent computer games or surfing the net.'

'Yes, Mrs Worthington, music is a source of pleasure and satisfaction for young people. I've seen your daughter respond with great pride when she works towards and achieves a set goal. Now she's ready to perform that piece, and may enjoy playing it to others. You'll be so proud of her on–stage at next month's recital.'

Helicopter parents

These hover over their offspring, jump to solve their problems, speak for them and against any and everyone who has the temerity to challenge them beyond their comfort zones. They have been described as hyper–present but psychologically absent. Their excess zeal and good intentions can rapidly become those of a control–freak. Their actions are counterproductive if the child does not develop independence and learn to solve their own challenges.

When such parents take over the teaching studio, the child relates to the parent rather than the teacher and is inhibited by the prospect of making mistakes. These adults rob children of the opportunity to work out their own way of doing things. They are better outside the studio door, contemplating how the toughest trees grow in the windiest conditions.

Overcommitted parents

These parents are overstretched financially and time–wise. Their commendable goal is to try to disengage their children from electronic babysitters. They keep them over–busy with a welter of sport, music, learning extension and clubs, while the financial cost strains the family budget. The offspring are reminded how fortunate they are to have so many opportunities, but the reality is 'less is more.' It is ironic that the things they do to benefit their children prevent them from spending quality time together. Such parents are so busy ensuring that they milk every possible drop from life, both for themselves and for their children, that they have little chance to digest it. They need to cut back, simplify and learn to say no.

In an effort to offer the best for their offspring, they may offer a bewildering array of choices and opportunities. Violinist Nicola Benedetti is a crusader for putting instruments into underprivileged children's' hands. She also believes that financially secure families lose the deep satisfaction of staying with one instrument and practising it to fulfilment. Then the real fun is experienced.

'A lot of the most privileged children face far too many choices,' said Benedetti. 'It is almost paralysing for children. It can disorient them like a constantly faulty light, flicking on and off.'

Benedetti said the controversial idea of a Tiger Mother – a determined parent who lays down challenges for their child – is not all bad. 'I was encouraged to be consistent with something and I wasn't allowed to change instruments. There is a balance to be struck, of course, but to me the most crucial thing is consistency if you ever want a child to have that feeling of satisfaction in their stomach when they have made something work because they stuck at it.' (Vanessa Thorpe, The Guardian, 5 May 2013)

Philistine parents

Some parents cripple their children's development with wisecracks about tunes the cow died on and questions like: 'Why do you need to practise so much? Haven't you learned it all yet?' Or: 'Be quiet, the neighbours will complain.' This may derive from jealousy that they lacked such opportunities in their early years and that the child may outstrip them.

Classic stories and excuses emerged in the course of a therapeutic Professional Development session I held with instrumental teachers. It transpired that we assume student reluctance is the reason for minimal practice, yet adults share the blame.

There were hilarious answers to the question: Why so little practice this week?

- A trumpeter was banished to play as far away as possible behind his house near the highway. His tentative tone was inhibited because truck drivers honked their horns at him.
- Another trumpeter had to play in the parked car, while his parents walked on the beach, because they were cowed by their duplex neighbours' aggressive complaints.
- A bull chased a red–haired saxophonist who was forced to play in the paddock.
- 'Mum's got a new boyfriend, so I have to live in a tent in the backyard.'
- 'Mum makes me play in the backyard, and it's been raining all week.'
- 'I do my practice in a cow paddock and a cow went off its brain and chased me.'
- 'Mum and Dad come home tired after work so they go mad at the noise.'

Toxic parent abuse

The other side of this is parents who expect excessive hours' practice. Legend has it that when the famous conductor Toscanini was a boy, his parents locked him in to practise for hours. So what could he do about going to the toilet? He had no option but to widdle in his cello.

Poor pianist Josef Hofman, aged 10, asked plaintively, 'What do they want to make a little boy like me work so hard for? I am not able to do it!' He was referring to 52 concerts in ten weeks! The New York Society for the Prevention of Cruelty to Children insisted on a medical examination that found signs of 'mental derangement'. A wealthy philanthropist then paid the father to keep Josef off the stage until he was 18.

Isaac Albeniz, a piano prodigy at four, was dragged along to perform dressed as a French musketeer, rapier and all. He ran away from home and became a street kid. Aged 12, he stowed away on a ship bound for Puerto Rico and supported himself by playing in saloons and on a lone recital tour from Cuba to San Francisco.

Problem parents

A teacher emailed me with a problem to which many would relate:

I hate conflict and find it difficult to deal with parents who take all their gripes out on me, the music teacher. When parents are fired up about something, I get shaky and can never defend myself. I always think afterwards that I should have handled it differently. I've tried the placid approach and also the 'you're not going to walk all over me' but nothing seems to work. Either way, the student is usually withdrawn from lessons because the parent disagrees with something:

- *I talk too much.*
- *The students play too much.*
- *The student wasn't given their fair share of my attention.*
- *I went mad at them for not doing enough practice.*
- *I'm too soft.*
- *I'm too hard.*

I've even been in trouble with a parent because I told her daughter to not talk to me in a disrespectful way! It's difficult to discuss this with colleagues as no one wants to admit that they are 'a bad teacher.'

She is not alone. When you suffer with obstructive parents, take heart—it could be worse. The Biker parent of a lazy, disruptive child threatened a teacher. The father left a vitriolic voice message for the teacher after he was forthright with the daughter. He warned the Principal that he and his Biker friends would block all the school exits in order to kick in the teacher's head that afternoon. Fortunately, 'I'd already learned a valuable lesson that if ever I give gentle or strong chastising words, I always write them down,' the teacher said. 'So I could show this register to the headmaster, who supported me and contacted Education Department personnel and the police. That afternoon, the law also waited at each school exit. 'But,' he says, 'I did feel hesitant leaving school on the following afternoons.' Another teacher told of being hit across his back with an umbrella by an elderly harridan who threatened: 'You lay off my granddaughter about all that practice.' As she huffed off, he yelled at her retreating back: 'But I don't even teach the girl.'

Keep a *'Glow File'* of students' and parents' positive letters and cards; jot down notes of supportive conversations. Read them when you feel depressed by conflict with parents. Remind yourself of those who thank you for your time and say they can't wait till next week. Of those who leave class early to get to music because they enjoy it so much.

Sylvia Griffiths wrote: 'I have a 16 year-old student who recently started singing lessons with me, and after her first lesson, when one of the things I did was answer her many questions, she said "That was the most exciting lesson I have ever had in my life". When I doubt my own teaching ability, I remember that.'Be yourself. Hold your head high. Trust in the value of your work. Infuse your personality into your teaching.

Chapter 35
Assert yourself with grace

Ways and words that win
Defuse anger and aggression with words that win. To build rapport, first:
LISTEN to understand the issue.
PAUSE to indicate your consideration.
BREATHE... then:
SPEAK low and slow.
- 'How can I help you?'
- 'I appreciate your point...'
- 'You're welcome to your opinion... however...'
- 'I hear what you say... but...' (i.e. even if I don't agree).

To disagree tactfully:
- 'Perhaps there's a misunderstanding'
- 'Maybe you missed my point, so let me clarify that again...'
- 'Let me check if I understood you correctly...' (Give them space to save face.)

Move to defuse issues
Open communication allows issues to be solved more quickly—and ensures resolution.

Frustrated by a student's laziness and refusal to fix core problems, I invented an innovative teaching tool. (Dare I share this?) As a visual reminder to alert clarinet students not to rest their arms on legs and hunch into banana backs, I attached innocuous tacks onto a hair band to place over the thigh. I had covered my back with an email beforehand but the daughter gave a lurid account of this instrument of torture, even though she could not have felt the slightest prick through her wool pullover. The parent took umbrage. The situation escalated with a flurry of cc emails to all and sundry including dire PDF attachments about duty of care. (How emails propagate and waste time!) Worn, I phoned to suggest a coffee. It took just an hour to reach mutual understanding; we parted with a hug and her daughter continued with clarinet lessons—until the following year when she turned to drama.

To handle confrontation:
- Stay close to the agenda.
- Use the inclusive 'we' form.
- 'I feel' is less confronting than 'You…'

Defuse aggression:
- Lower voice (hum).
- 'Down–talk' at ends of sentences.
- Slow down.
- Be objective.
- Create win–win situations.
- De–personalise.

If the issue becomes a time–waster:

'I appreciate your time…' 'I realise you're busy…' 'Let's follow up next week.'
Avoid aggressive 'you' talk which may escalate aggression.
Aim to create win–win outcomes.
'I understand/I'm confident that/I feel that...'
'I hear what you say but dxvjefdlkj...you have a point but dxvjefdlkj... I agree in part but dxvjefdlkj.' (This is the rutted LP record technique.)
Shoulders down, head high, breathe—and smile!

Consider gender communication styles

While we hesitate to generalise along gender lines, it may be helpful to consider how communication styles can differ between males and females. The following is adapted from Candy Tymson's *Gender Games*.

MALE STYLE FOCUS	FEMALE STYLE FOCUS
On information	On relationships
Report style speaking	Rapport style speaking
Goal driven	Process oriented
Single-task approach	Multi-tasking approach
Succinct language	Story-telling style
Working towards a destination	On a journey
Need to know the answers	Want to ask the right questions

MALE DIRECT STYLE	FEMALE INDIRECT STYLE
Dominate others in discussion	Engage in discussion
Ask questions to reinforce status	Ask questions to encourage discussion
State opinions in absolute way	Express opinions tentatively
Focus on the task	Focus on people/relationships

WHEN HE HAS A PROBLEM	WHEN SHE HAS A PROBLEM
Appears to shut-down	Wants to talk
Retreats into himself	Seeks colleagues' help
Wants to be 'left alone'	Openly discusses issues
Needs to work it out for himself	Just wants the right outcome

Body language signals can differ between male and female. For example in discussion, a nod of the head:

MALE	FEMALE
'I've made a decision'	'I'm listening, I hear what you say.'

We educators are professionals and deserve respect. Ask and you shall receive.
No one can make you feel inferior without your consent.
– Eleanor Roosevelt

Chapter 36

Speak out with confidence in parent–teacher meetings

The new school year has settled in and all too soon come the dreaded PT meetings. What is worse than a wriggling audience of reluctant school kids? Answer: Their parents.

All those eyes are fixed on the hapless teacher, assessing: will this person see the hidden talents in my precious child?

Have you sometimes experienced a few nerves on the night? Shaky voice, dry mouth and gasping for air? Presentation anxiety is the Number One Fear in society above those of flying, dying and bankruptcy, according to the Book of Lists. It's normal—and you are not defenceless. Here are some simple preparations that you can do in the privacy of your car while driving to school. A few red lights can be put to excellent use to build your confident presentation.

First, let's look at the source of the problem. When we're under pressure in basic survival mode, the Primitive Reptilian brain takes over, initiating and regulating the Fight–or–Flight response. Neither fight nor flight is appropriate behaviour in front of the parents. All those unsettling symptoms of excess adrenaline rush are bred here, as the brain stem regulates:

- Heartbeat; as this races, so we tend to rush our speech
- Breathing becomes strained, shallow

- Equilibrium and muscle tone, hence the wobbly knees and shaky hands.

The secret is to channel the adrenaline into energy, and by tapping back into the cerebral cortex, all those unpleasant symptoms fall away. How? It's simple.

At the red lights, or when you park in the grounds, take a few moments to breathe deep and slow. This is enhanced by placing a hand on your forehead, in Brain–Gym terminology known as the 'positive points'. This curbs excess fight or flight response, releases your memory box (you've seen students do this when asked a question and they say: 'It's on the tip of my tongue') and allows full frontal lobe thinking. A bonus is that this links to the stomach's emotional stress–release points, calming queasiness.

Shrill or thin voice? To warm–up your voice hum along to the radio as you drive. This counters any tendencies for high–pitched, thin tone. Open your throat with a yawn (thus bringing in the 'inspiration' of vital oxygen) or a laugh. Ensure an interesting range of modulation by humming siren type noises, up and down. Relax tight lips and jaw by making motorbike type 'brmm–brmm' noises. (But first, check for cars in the next lane, in case a student's mother is eying you with interest.)

Dry mouth? Stress can cause dehydration. This is unfortunate for speakers, as the vocal folds need fluid to vibrate freely and resonate with good projection. Water is also a brain–food, enabling us to think fast on our feet. The electrical and chemical actions of the central nervous system and brain depend on efficient conduction—via fluid—of electrical currents to pass messages between the brain and sensory organs.

Reach for your water bottle at the red lights. Increase your water intake in the days before. Think positive thoughts.

Walk around the block before the session. If you feel an instinct to pace the floor before the parents arrive, don't curb it; this instinctive reaction gets blood circulating, and the 'cross–crawl' action activates whole–brain thought.

A few drops of the homoeopathic Dr Bach Rescue Remedy under your tongue can aid centring and focus as well as alleviate panic, exhaustion, tiredness and fear. It is available at health stores and many pharmacists.

http://www.bachflower.com/rescue-remedy-information/.

✜

The parents are about to arrive. Take another slow, deep breath. Stand against a wall to counter that instinctive defensive hunching of posture.

- When meeting new parents create a positive first impression with:
- Upright posture.
- Handshake—firm but don't crush.
- Have the courage to look people in the eye.
- Use their names in conversation.
- Smile (where appropriate)—it warms the voice.
- Stand tall. You fulfil an excellent role in shaping the lives of young people.
- If you suffer a bout of 'brain–fog' during the question time, casually pause, say 'Hmm, that's a good question' while you thoughtfully place a hand on your forehead. The pause adds gravitas and credibility, and gives you time to think and poise.
- Smile.
- Breathe.
- Slow down.
- Communicate with your listeners.

Chapter 37

Your voice is your instrument–handle with care

Talking over articulate, assertive young people may strain teachers' voices. There is added pressure for music teachers who switch between speaking and singing voices and their different projection techniques. As well as classes they may direct choirs, orchestras and bands of frisky children. Adjudicating competitions, giving seminars or even teaching one–to–one for long days can be wearing. Add to that the chance of picking up infections that circulate.

This is a tip to avoid voice malfunction:

Singers and speakers should maintain healthy mucous membranes by drinking plenty of water—two or three litres each day—to hydrate their vocal folds. Steam inhalation is also a wonderful remedy for infection. You can purchase a simple plastic steam inhaler for a few dollars at a pharmacist. Or cover your head with a towel over a basin of steaming water. (It's also a great facial!)

The 'Entertainer's Secret Throat Relief' spray promises rapid relief of hoarse voice, laryngitis, dry throat and vocal strain.

https://www.entertainers-secret.com.au/store/

All power to your voice

Teachers of classes and ensembles often have to quieten unruly students. Dealing with unreceptive audiences can strain the voice. A solution is to use a technique called oral 'twang' or 'safe yelling.' To do this take a short, high breath, brace your torso, retract the false vocal folds (for example with a social yawn) and make spontaneous loud sounds. An example of this is the happy yell of Italian mamas when they call out for the children and papa to come for dinner—'mangiamo!' Or a child's 'Muuuum.'

Can you recall a noisy party where one voice can be heard over all the rest?

The difference is the amount of 'twang' or 'ringing' quality in the voice, a sound made by tightening the collar of the laryngeal tube, which creates another resonator within the vocal tract. The extra resonance in the 2 to 4 kilohertz band of the sound spectrum contributes to the perception of loudness or 'ringing' tone. Activate this twang quality to protect your voice in noisy environments and enable you to be heard more easily without vocal trauma.

Ensure Free Speech

Have you ever opened your mouth to speak in public, or to sing, and nothing comes out? The sound seems to jam up in your throat? Here's a simple solution to free your voice as you drive to your presentation.

First, let's understand why this unnerving experience might occur. When under threat or pressure, we instinctively tighten our muscles. As our throat, jaw, vocal folds and larynx tense, our voice simply shuts down or becomes thin, even squeaky.

Many have experienced the 'false' vocal folds' role in protecting us from choking; remember at that barbecue when a mosquito or moth flew into your mouth. Your false vocal folds instinctively clamped shut to stop the insect from choking you. In a performance situation, the false folds misread our defensive tension and try to protect us from perceived threat, by clamping shut and closing down our vocal apparatus. Thanks a lot!

The solution is simple. And you can do this driving in your car to school. Just yawn. Most effective is the beginning part of it—the whole sabre-tooth tiger bit isn't necessary.

Or you could sing along to some opera on your car sound system; those full blooded sobs and laughs are perfect for opening the vocal folds, which is one reason why opera singers can project in huge auditoria without amplification.

Or indulge in a loud, jolly Santa Ho ho ho' as you drive along. But choose your moments. This is not recommended if there are bikers in the next lane. Coping with road rage is hardly confidence building just before speaking!

Just before you walk on stage or in the classroom, ensure your voice will project with confidence by yawning a very subtle social yawn.

Create a voice that's music to listeners' ears

- Lower your voice with a hum.
- Create 'down–talk' at ends of sentences. If you notice 'up–talk' remember to lower at the next full stop. You have just turned a negative into a positive by widening your range.
- Pause to empower.
- Breathe! Breathe to highlight an important point; after a breath your voice is stronger.

CODA

Music teachers can take credit for enriching students' lives, opening their minds and ears to beauty and for giving them scope to express their imagination. In the process they help create rounded, productive and fine human beings who enhance our society.

Never let anyone demean your teaching by suggesting that teachers are 'failed performers'. Such people are blind to the far-reaching influence which can be exerted by teachers. Some musicians gained far more impressive reputations as teachers than they would have as performers. Athough an excellent violinist, Carl Flesch was less confident onstage. But his repute towers as a leading string pedagogue. Manuel Garcia had a pleasant voice, but feared losing it in performances. Eventually, he did damage it through overwork. He devoted himself to his main love, teaching. Without this sobering experience, would he have had the wisdom to guide Jenny Lind through a rest and technical program which saved her voice?

If our students learn to love and enjoy their music our teaching is worthwhile, however many stumbles along the way. Think through memories of your former teachers. This one insisted on endless exercises. That old–school dragon balanced pennies on your hands and hit your fingers with a pencil or ruler when they fell off, or you played wrong notes.

Another played recordings, planned concerts and chamber music sessions. Listened to your troubles and encouraged that better tims lay ahead. Which was the 'best' teacher?

Balance is essential. We must remember to teach the art, not just technique. Many institutions, systems and teachers appear to bow and sacrifice in a misguided attempt to appease the insatiable monster, 'technique', mistaking it for the soul–enriching values of the arts. Even worse, the pursuit of perfection has dampened many artists' sheer love of beauty and ability to express the depth of feeling and meaning.

Pianist Anna Goldsworthy wrote a memoir, *Piano Lessons*. Her account of a decade's relationship between student and piano teacher Eleonora Sivan is honest and often moving. Imagine if someone wrote about their experiences of learning with you, what might they say?

Publishers' Weekly wrote:

At first Sivan did not believe that Goldsworthy had the "emotional freedom" to be a concert pianist. However, the youth proved her wrong by incorporating her teacher's radiant artistry and coming to feel the joy of playing. Moreover, after earning top prizes and attaining her dream of playing a Beethoven concerto with a full orchestra, Goldsworthy returned the gift of music by teaching, as per Sivan's ministrations, and composing to her teacher this rich, heartfelt tribute.

When teachers maintain positive communication and interaction with students and parents, musical results soar, and lessons reap rewards. In the grind of timetables, rehearsals, prodding students and fending off tough parents, music teachers deserve encouragement and appreciation.

At the tea break in Brisbane Symphony Orchestra rehearsal I asked my colleagues 'What are your top tips for teachers?' Thank you for these responses:

- 'Mix it up, change the room, keep them on their toes…
- Be flexible; run with what you have.' (Karina Bryer)
- 'Involve yourself with hobbies or ensembles away from the school…
- Remember, you're responsible for the input, but not the end result, especially if students don't practise. You can control the input but not the output.' (Matthew Hoey)
- 'You catch more flies with honey than with vinegar. Chastising just turns students off. If a lesson is enjoyable and fun, they will even face scales. (Alicia Ninnes)

To my question 'What makes teachers' work positive, fruitful, even enjoyable? What helps you get up in the mornings and go back to the coalface?'

- The studio concert when pupils have prepared and achieved...

The most rewarding are the kids who struggle and it seems they just don't get it. Then, if it's perhaps suggested they stop learning, they're horrified. I'm surprised to find how important music is to them.' (Tertia Hogan)
- 'It's great when students practise and it all comes together. They initially don't hear much of the detail that the teacher does, but when it comes together they suddenly realise what they can achieve.' (Allan Hall)
- 'My pupils succeed because I don't yell; I don't force them into exams. I listen and treat them as people.' (Alicia Ninnes)
- 'To be an inspirational teacher for the musicians of the future.' (Antoni Bonetti)
- 'Music is powerful. It is food for the Soul. If I can assist just one person to find what music is to them, then it is all worthwhile.' (Tertia Hogan)
- John Curro reflects: 'The mark of a really effective teacher is surely the ability to lead the student, as quickly as possible, to the point where the teacher is no longer needed.'
- David Shephard sums up his experience as both pupil and teacher: 'My teacher was always encouraging and positive and I have held him in the highest regard all my life. I think it a great privilege and responsibility to be entrusted with students, many of tender age, and seeing your ideas taking root and bearing fruit.'

For many students, music lessons are springs of rejuvenation in the desert patches of their lives. They can express pent–up emotions in a range of sounds. Those who have to live with critical parents or in dysfunctional homes look forward to weekly one–on–one interaction with a positive, understanding and listening adult.

Many will look back, decades later, and remember the words you spoke, the times you listened, and how your lessons changed their lives.

You help them blossom in arid times. Your excellent work is valued! Bravo!

Music washes away from the soul the dust of everyday life.
– Red Auerbach

Without music, life is a journey through a desert.
–Pat Conroy

Bibliography

Berlioz, Hector, *Memoirs from 1803-1865*, ed. Ernest Newman (Dover Publications, 1932)

Bonetti, Ruth, *Confident Music Performance* (Words and Music, 2003, 2002011)

Bonetti, Ruth, *Don't Freak Out – Speak Out* (Words and Music, 2001, 2003, 2005, 2010)

Bonetti, Ruth, *Enjoy Playing the Clarinet* (Oxford University Press, 1985, 1997)

Bonetti, Ruth, *Practice is a Dirty Word; How to clean up your act* (Words and Music, 2002, 2005, 2006, 2007, 2011)

Bonetti, Ruth, *Practice WAS a Dirty Word; Practice Journal* (Words and Music, 2007, 2011)

Chapman, Gary, *Five Love Languages; The secret to love that lasts* (Northfield Press, 2010)

Colwell, Richard J. and Michael P. Hewitt, *The Teaching of Instrumental Music* 4th ed. (Boston: Prentice Hall, 2011)

Dennison, Paul E. and Dennison, Gail E., *Brain Gym: Teachers' Edition* (California, Edu-Kinesthetics Inc. 1989 and 1994)

Choksy, Lois, *The Kodály Method 1*, 3rd ed. (Upper Saddle River, NJ: Prentice Hall, 1999)

Duval, David, *The World of the Concert Pianist* (Victor Gollancz, 1985)

Fink, Henry T., *Success in Music and How It is Won* (Charles Scribners' Sons, 1909)

Gardner, H., & Hatch, T. (1989). 'Multiple intelligences go to school: Educational implications of the theory of multiple intelligences.' *Educational Researcher, 18* (8), 4-9

Goldsworthy, Anna, *Piano Lessons* (Black Inc, 2009)

Hamburger, Michael, transl. *Ludwig Beethoven, Letters, Journals and Conversations* (Jonathan Cape, 1966)

Hannaford, Carla, *Smart Moves: Why learning is not all in your head* (Great Ocean, Arlington, Virginia 1995)

Kahn, Albert E., *Joys and Sorrows - Pablo Casals* (Eel Pie Publishing, 1970)

Kirk, H.L., *Pablo Casals: A biography* (Hutchinson and Co., 1994)

Leunig, Michael, *The Prayer Tree* (HarperCollins, 1990)

Lim, Anne, 'Playing for Keeps', *Australian Weekly Review*, April 23-4, 1994

Littauer, Florence, *Personality Plus: How to Understand Others by Understanding Yourself* (Revell; Rev/Expand September 01 1992)

Mair, George, *Bette; An Intimate Biography of Bette Midler* (New York, Birch Lane Press, 1995)

Mark, Michael L. and Madura, Patrice, *Music Education in Your Hands; An Introduction for future teachers* (New York, Routledge: 2010)

Martin, Ben, *Marcel Marceau: Master of Mime* (UK: Paddington Press Limited, 1978)

Morrison, Bryce, 'Practising? I never do any', *Observer Magazine*, 10 November, 1974

Moore, Gerald, *Am I Too Loud?* (Penguin, 1962)

Mozart, Wolfgang Amadeus, *Mozart's Letters: An Illustrated Selection* (London, Barrie & Jenkins, 1990)

Newman, Ernest, *The Man Liszt* (Victor Gollancz, 1970)

Jean Piaget, *The Origins of Intelligence in Children* (New York: W.W.Norton and Company, Inc., 1963)

Prensky, Marc, *Don't Bother Me Mom–I'm Learning!* (St Paul, MN: Paragon House Publishers, 2006)

Rudolph, Thomas and James Frankel, *You Tube in Music Education* (New York: Hal Leonard, 2009)

Riso, Don Richard and Hudson, Russ, *The Wisdom of the Enneagram* (Bantam Books, 1999)

Schafer, Murray A., *The Thinking Ear* (Toronto: Arcana Editions, 1988)

Shaw, George Bernard, *Shaw's Music: The Complete Musical Criticism of Bernard Shaw* (The Bodley Head, Paperback, 1989. 8vo. 3 vols. Second Revised Edition)

Scholes, Percy, *The Oxford Companion to Music* (Oxford: Oxford University Press, 1970.)

Schonberg, Harold C., *The Great Pianists* (London: Victor Gollancz, 1964)

Spohr, Louis, *Autobiography*, Frederick Freeman, *(ed.)*, (Da Capo Press, 1969)

Suzuki, Shinichi, *Nurtured by Love; The classic approach to talent education* (Smithtown, NY: Exposition Press, 1983)

Thorpe, Vanessa, 'Stick to one instrument, violinist Benedetti tells pushy parents.' *The Guardian*, 5 May 2013

Tymson, Candy, *Gender Games; Doing business with the opposite sex* (Sydney: Tymson Communications, 1998)

Walker, Alan, (ed.), *Robert Schumann: the Man and his Music* (London: Barrie and Jenkins, Ltd., 1972)

Websites

Alexander Technique: http://www.alexandertechnique.com/
A Music Education Blog Collective: http://collective.musiced.net/
American Choral Directors Association: www.acda.org
American String Teachers Association: www.asta.org
Bookstore, Juilliard: http://www.bookstore.juilliard.edu/
Brain Gym/Educational Kinesiology Foundation: http://www.braingym.org/
British Music Society: www.musicweb.uk.net/BMS
Classical Music Archives: http://www.classicalmusicarchives.com
Classical Music search engine: classicalsearch.com
Composers, analysis: www.musicaltimes.co.uk
Classics for Kids: http://www.classicsforkids.com/index.asp
Conductors Guild: www.conductorsguild.org
For theory worksheets and games see:
http://www.musicfun.net.au/worksheets.htm
http://www.musicfun.net.au/pdf_files/about_notes.pdf
http://www.pianimation.com/teacher-resources/free-games/
IMSLP Petrucci Music Library: http://imslp.org/
International Society for Improvised Music (ISIM)
International Suzuki Association www.suzukiassociation.org
K-12 Resources for Music Educators: http://www.k-12music.org/
MENC http://www.MENC.com/
Music resources - Music on the Move: www.motm.com.au
  Out of Print Music and Books: www.sheetmusicwarehouse.
The Enneagram: http://www.enneagraminstitute.com/

The Four Temperaments: http://www.kheper.net/topics/typology/four_humours.html
Multiple Intelligences: http://www.infed.org/thinkers/gardner.htm
National Association for Music Education:http://www.nafme.org/
Teachnology: http://www.teach-nology.com
The American Educational Research Foundation (AERA) www.aera.net
The American Federation of Teachers www.aft.org
The Choral Public Domain Library: http://www.cpdl.org
The National Education Association www.nea.org
Music enhances brain function: http://www.trumusic.com/musicgen.htm
http://www.amcmusic.com/pubpol/weinberger.html
National Band Association http://www.nationalbandassociation.org
Pareto 80/20 Principle: http://www.gassner.co.il/p

Index

A

Abreu, Jose 154
Albeniz, Isaac 181
Allegar, John 118
Applied Kinesiology 49, 109
Arrau, Claudio 9, 169

B

Baxter, Daniel 92
Beek, Tom 96, 100
Beethoven, Ludwig van 32, 35, 38, 102, 107, 108, 110, 132, 134, 163, 193
Berlioz, Hector 129, 132, 135
Brain Gym 48, 109, 119, 160
breath 15, 46, 113, 115, 117, 120, 140, 151, 154, 156, 188, 190, 191

C

Cameron, Julia 45
Casals, Pablo 166, 168, 172
Chapman, Gary 87
Copyright ii, 63, 64
Crews, Rita 13, 27
Cuddeford, James 170
Curro, John, 67, 68, 194

D

Dalcroze Method 92, 146
Davis, Phil 98
Dennison, Paul E. and Gail 109

E

El Sistema, 154, 155
Emotional Freedom Technique 52, 55, 117, 121

F

Fay, Amy 9

G

Goldsworthy, Anna 193
Gough, Sue 130

H

Hebden, Barbara 131
Helfgott, David 169
Hofman, Josef 181

J

Joyce, Cheryl 7

K

Kodály Method 8, 146

L

Liszt, Franz 9, 11, 128, 171, 177

M

Marceau, Marcel 136
Mendelssohn, Felix 171
Midler, Bette 136
Moore, Gerald 115
Morrow, Cheryl 154, 155, 162, 163
Mother Theresa 81
Mozart, Leopold 167, 168
Mozart. Wolfgang 61, 62, 110, 132, 154, 163

O

Olding, Dene 169, 170

P

Page, Pamela 169
Pareto Principle (80/20) 72
Piaget, Jean 79
Positive Points 49, 119, 121, 160, 161, 187
Price, Julie v, 164

R

Redman, Jason 127
relaxation 12, 46, 51
Relaxation techniques 12
Rubenstein 134, 172

S

Schumann, Clara 34, 168
Schumann, Robert 11, 34, 83, 129, 131, 132, 168
Shaw, George Bernard 68, 129, 131
Shephard, David 12, 194
Spohr, Louis 107, 108, 133, 134
Suzuki, Shinichi 146, 147, 153, 174

T

Thorpe, Vanessa 180

Here are the tools for **Star Performance!**
Books & Workshops
by Ruth Bonetti

Confident Music Performance
They've practised, they're talented, but still public performance is an ordeal for many. This resource for musicians, teachers and parents helps pupils prepare, conquer nerves and shine onstage. It gives solutions for those unsettling shakes, dry mouth and memory lapses that can unnerve even experienced performers. This book offers practical, holistic solutions for all aspects of performance anxiety.

Practice is a Dirty Word – How to clean up your act
A half-hour music lesson = 0.3% of a student's week. Here's how to reinforce the other 99.7%
• Set and reach goals
• Plan practice time
• Problem-solve tricky bars
• Face and master scales
• Retain standard in busy times
• Revive enthusiasm and excel in exams and recitals
This book rescues teachers, parents and students from the bogey of practice.
Young musicians will enjoy playing and realise their potential.

Grade 7 student reviews of *Practice is a Dirty Word*:
"This is a 'MUST READ' for anyone like me who hates to learn but loves music."
"A great book for people who just hate to practise."
"This book was easy to read and it helped me a lot with my everyday life. It has worked wonders. It made me change my mind completely about practising and now I am enjoying and playing better all thanks to Ruth Bonetti."
"What I found most useful were tips for rehearsing with the accompanist,

ways to have self-esteem, and that a small mistake isn't major doom!"
"The book affected me tremendously and helped me practise even better than usual. I really enjoyed this book, it would do wonders for you."

Practice WAS a Dirty Word – Music Journal

Ruth Bonetti's innovative practice diary encourages students to take ownership of their
time, development and progress, to maximise their talent.
Weekly motivational tips highlight techniques learned in Practice is a Dirty Word. Students – as well as teachers and parents – have space to plan repertoire, set and review goals and brainstorm ways to achieve results. Students can enjoy music and shine in performance.
"Ruth Bonetti has inspired me. I'm off to make music."
– Good Reading
"Practice tips with some real gems of information and advice. I particularly liked the 'High 5'. The concept is that you play tricky sections 5 times on 5 days between lessons to get them cracked."
– Mike Saville, www.howtopractice.com

Speak Out – Don't Freak Out

Public Speaking With Confidence.
This invaluable guide for speakers covers all aspects of preparation – mental, emotional, physical and presentation.
A must for all who stand up and speak in public.
Available also as audio Cd and e-book at
www.ruthbonetti.com
"Clearly written, to the point and well set out, this book represents great value for money. I recommend it wholeheartedly."
– Writing Queensland

What critics and readers say about Ruth Bonetti's books…

"Specific advice and clear explanations are a boon after years of being told to 'stay calm' without being told how, of being told 'you'll be fine' by people who don't perform themselves."
– NSW Association for the Gifted and Talented

"Thank you from the core of my heart for illuminating me with techniques to overcome stage fear. I am very grateful!"
– Sandeep Harish, India

"Stimulating, thought provoking, and engagingly written by an experienced professional musician and music teacher, this is a highly recommended volume for music teachers, parents and music students." – Accessed

"Your books are so good they should be bottled!"
– Dr Anna Burrows, The Gap, Australia

"A healing, compassionate little book."
– Margery Smith, Lecturer, University of Newcastle, Australia

"This easy to read, gem of a publication gives lots of practical, down-to-earth advice … written in a sympathetic, user friendly style, it is highly recommended." – Dr Rita Crews, The Studio

"This book is a Godsend! Can you imagine never again having to nag your student to practise? This book could be the end of all your woes!" – Mary Nemet, Strings USA

"It is mandatory reading for all would-be performers, seasoned or otherwise." – Stringendo

"Bonetti's perceptive and positive approach will be beneficial to any musician." – Winds, UK

"So helpful and inspiring that I now incorporate its principles into my performing and teaching. This book is truly a needed resource in this day of beta-blockers and high-pressure audition situations. I know of no other book that addresses this issue in such an engaging manner. It is essential equipment for any musician, professional or student."
– Mary Natvig, PhD, Associate Professor
Bowling Green State university, Ohio, US

For information about Ruth Bonetti's books,
to order copies or arrange workshops:
www.ruthbonetti.com
email: ruth@ruthbonetti.com
Ph: (61 7) 3300 2286 or 0411 782 404

Ruth Presents:
WORKSHOPS / MASTER CLASSES FOR STUDENTS
Include:
- How to Practise for Success
- How to Impress the Examiner – and Excel
- Scales and Arpeggios Demystified
- 7 Easy Habits for Confident Performance
- Prepare for Confident Oral Presentations
- Enjoy Playing the Clarinet

Days of Excellence Program (Choose modules to suit your program)
WORKSHOPS FOR MUSIC TEACHERS
Topics include:
- How to Motivate, Retain and Inspire Students
- Professional Parent-Teacher Communication
- Prepare Students for Confident Performance
- Empower Students to Realise Performance Potential

TALK FOR PARENTS
- Help your Child Excel with Music

From her perspective as an AMEB examiner, educator and mother of three sons, Ruth solves common issues such as:
"How can I enforce boring practice?"
"Should I sit in on lessons?"
"How to ease performance stress?"
"My child has talent but has lost interest! How do I rekindle their enjoyment?"

"Ruth Bonetti was a faculty asset far beyond our expectations. Students responded so positively to her coaching and vibrant personality that we had to expand her workload and schedule additional sessions. I cannot say

enough positive about Mrs Bonetti's work as a performance coach."
Dr Victor E. Gebauer, executive director, Lutheran Music Program, Minneapolis, USA

"Ruth delighted the participants with her infectious good humour and vibrant personality. Her presentations were a highlight due to Ruth's ability to involve everyone, her enthusiasm and charisma."
Malcolm F. Potter, President, Music Teachers

www.ingramcontent.com/pod-product-compliance
Lightning Source LLC
Chambersburg PA
CBHW051429290426
44109CB00016B/1491